THE YALE SHAKESPEARE

Revised Edition

General Editors

Helge Kökeritz and Charles T. Prouty

Published on the fund

given to the Yale University Press in 1917

by the members of the

Kingsley Trust Association

(Scroll and Key Society of Yale College)

to commemorate the seventy-fifth anniversary

of the founding of the society

THE YALE SHAKESPEARE

TWELFTH NIGHT
OR WHAT YOU WILL

Edited by William P. Holden

NEW HAVEN AND LONDON:

YALE UNIVERSITY PRESS

Preface of the General Editors

AS the late Professor Tucker Brooke has observed, practically all modern editions of Shakespeare are 18th-century versions of the plays, based on the additions, alterations, and emendations of editors of that period. It has been our purpose, as it was Professor Brooke's, to give the modern reader Shakespeare's plays in the approximate form of their original appearance.

About half the plays appeared in quarto form before the publication of the First Folio in 1623. Thus for a large number of plays the only available text is that of the Folio. In the case of quarto plays our policy has been to use that text as the basis of the edition, unless it is clear that the text has been contaminated.

Interesting for us today is the fact that there are no act or scene divisions in the Quartos with the exception of *Othello*, which does mark Acts I, II, IV, and V but lacks indications of scenes. Even in the Folio, although act divisions are generally noted, only a part of the scenes are divided. In no case, either in Quarto or Folio, is there any indication of the place of action. The manifold scene divisions for the battle in such a play as *Antony and Cleopatra*, together with such locations as "Another part of the field," are the additions of the 18th century.

We have eliminated all indications of the place and time of action, because there is no authority for them in the originals and because Shakespeare gives such information, when it is requisite for understanding the play, through the dialogue of the actors. We have been sparing in our use of added scene and, in some cases, act divisions, because these frequently impede the flow of the action, which in Shakespeare's time was curiously like that of modern films.

Spelling has been modernized except when the original clearly indicates a pronunciation unlike our own, e.g. *desart* (desert), *divel* (devil), *banket* (banquet), and often in such Elizabethan syncopations as *ere* (e'er), *stolne* (stol'n), and *tane* (ta'en). In reproducing such forms we have followed the inconsistent usage of the original.

We have also preserved much more of the original capitalization than is usual, for often this is a part of the meaning. In like manner we have tended to adopt the lineation of the original in many cases where modern editors print prose as verse or verse as prose. We have, moreover, followed the original punctuation wherever it was practicable.

In verse we print a final *-ed* to indicate its full syllabic value, otherwise *'d*. In prose we have followed the inconsistencies of the original in this respect.

Our general practice has been to include in footnotes all information a reader needs for immediate understanding of the given page. In somewhat empiric fashion we repeat glosses as we think the reader needs to be reminded of the meaning. Further information is given in notes (indicated by the letter *N* in the footnotes) to be found at the back of each volume. Appendices deal with the text and sources of the play.

Square brackets indicate material not found in the original text. Long emendations or lines taken from another authoritative text of a play are indicated in the footnotes for the information of the reader. We have silently corrected obvious typographical errors.

CONTENTS

[THE ACTORS' NAMES

ORSINO, DUKE OF ILLYRIA
SEBASTIAN, *brother to Viola*
ANTONIO, *a sea captain, friend to Sebastian*
A SEA CAPTAIN, *friend to Viola*
VALENTINE ⎫
CURIO ⎭ *gentlemen attending on the Duke*
SIR TOBY BELCH, *kinsman of Olivia*
SIR ANDREW AGUECHEEK, *suitor of Olivia*
MALVOLIO, *steward to Olivia*
FABIAN, *an attendant to Olivia*
THE CLOWN FESTE, *Olivia's fool*

OLIVIA, *a countess*
VIOLA, *in love with the Duke; sister to Sebastian*
MARIA, *Olivia's gentlewoman*

Lords, a Priest, Sailors, Officers, Musicians, and other
  Attendants

Scene: Illyria and the coast nearby]

[The Actors' . . . nearby] N.

TWELFTH NIGHT

OR WHAT YOU WILL

Act I

SCENE 1

*Enter Orsino, Duke of Illyria, Curio, and
other Lords.*

Duke. If music be the food of love, play on!
Give me excess of it, that surfeiting,
The appetite may sicken and so die.
That strain agen! It had a dying fall;
O, it came o'er my ear like the sweet sound   5
That breathes upon a bank of violets,
Stealing and giving odor. Enough, no more;
'Tis not so sweet now as it was before.
O spirit of love, how quick and fresh art thou,
That notwithstanding thy capacity,   10
Receiveth as the sea. Nought enters there,
Of what validity and pitch soe'er,
But falls into abatement and low price
Even in a minute. So full of shapes is fancy
That it alone is high fantastical.   15
Curio. Will you go hunt, my lord?

1–3 If music . . . so die N. 4 **agen** again. **fall cadence,**
rhythm. 5 **sound** both the sound of music and of the wind.
9–14 O spirit . . . in a minute N. 9 **quick** alive. 12 **pitch** high
point of a falcon's flight. 14 **Even** monosyllabic. **shapes** figures,
forms. **fancy** imagination, the mind of the lover N. 15 **high fantastical** highly changeable and imaginative.

1

Duke.   What, Curio?
Curio. The hart.
Duke. Why, so I do, the noblest that I have.
O, when mine eyes did see Olivia first,
Methought she purg'd the air of pestilence.   20
That instant was I turn'd into a hart,
And my desires like fell and cruel hounds
Ere since pursue me. How now, what news from her?

Enter Valentine.

Valentine. So please my lord, I might not be ad-
        mitted,
But from her handmaid do return this answer: 25
The element itself, till seven years' heat,
Shall not behold her face at ample view;
But like a cloistress she will veiled walk,
And water once a day her chamber round
With eye-offending brine: all this to season   30
A brother's dead love, which she would keep fresh
And lasting in her sad remembrance.
Duke. O, she that hath a heart of that fine frame
To pay this debt of love but to a brother,
How will she love when the rich golden shaft   35
Hath kill'd the flock of all affections else
That live in her; when liver, brain, and heart,
These sovereign thrones, are all supplied and fill'd,

17 **hart** the adult male deer. 18 **the noblest** N. 20 **Methought** it
seemed to me. 21 **hart** possibly a pun on 'heart' N. 22 **fell** savage,
fierce. 23 **Ere** e'er, ever. 24 **might not** could not. 26 **element** sky.
heat the course of the sun. 28 **cloistress** nun in a convent. 30 **eye-
offending brine** the salt tears irritate the eye. **to season** both 'to
spice' and 'to preserve.' 32 **remembrance** probably four syllables.
33 **frame** construction. 35 **golden shaft** Cupid's golden arrow
brings love N. 36 **else** other. 37 **liver, brain, and heart** supposed
centers of love, thought, and emotion, respectively.

Her sweet perfections, with one self king.
Away before me to sweet beds of flow'rs;   **40**
Love-thoughts lie rich when canopied with bow'rs.

                                     Exeunt.

SCENE 2

Enter Viola, a Captain, and Sailors.

Viola. What country, friends, is this?
Captain. This is Illyria, lady.
Viola. And what should I do in Illyria?
My brother he is in Elysium.   4
Perchance he is not drown'd. What think you sailors?
  Captain. It is perchance that you yourself were
    sav'd.
  Viola. O my poor brother, and so perchance may
    he be!
  Captain. True, madam, and to comfort you with
    chance,
Assure yourself, after our ship did split,   9
When you, and those poor number sav'd with you,
Hung on our driving boat, I saw your brother,
Most provident in peril, bind himself
(Courage and hope both teaching him the practice)
To a strong mast that liv'd upon the sea:
Where, like Arion on the dolphin's back,   15
I saw him hold acquaintance with the waves
So long as I could see.

39 **one self king** one and the same person, her husband. 3 **Illyria** on the east coast of the Adriatic. 4 **Elysium** heaven (Greek mythology) N. 8 **chance** what may have happened. 11 **driving** 'driving before the wind' or 'drifting.' 12 **provident** foreseeing and thrifty. 14 **liv'd** survived by floating. 15 **Arion** F *Orion* N.

Viola. For saying so, there's gold.
Mine own escape unfoldeth to my hope,
Whereto thy speech serves for authority   20
The like of him. Know'st thou this country?
Captain. Ay, madam, well, for I was bred and born
Not three hours' travel from this very place.
Viola. Who governs here?
Captain. A noble duke in nature as in name.   25
Viola. What is his name?
Captain. Orsino.
Viola. Orsino. I have heard my father name him.
He was a bachelor then.
Captain. And so is now, or was so very late: 30
For but a month ago I went from hence,
And then 'twas fresh in murmur (as you know
What great ones do, the less will prattle of)
That he did seek the love of fair Olivia.
Viola. What's she?   35
Captain. A virtuous maid, the daughter of a count
That died some twelvemonth since; then leaving her
In the protection of his son, her brother,
Who shortly also died; for whose dear love,
They say, she hath abjur'd the sight   40
And company of men.
Viola.   O that I serv'd that lady,
And might not be deliver'd to the world
Till I had made mine own occasion mellow,

19 **unfoldeth to my hope** reveals itself so as to give me hope (for
my brother). 21 **the like** the same escape. **country** probably three
syllables. 22 **bred** conceived. 32 **'twas fresh in murmur** there was
a current rumor. 35 **What's she** 'who's she' and 'what sort of
person is she.' 42 **deliver'd** given over to, disclosed, revealed N.
43 **Till . . . mellow** till I had arranged my own proper opportunity (to disclose).

What my estate is.

Captain. That were hard to compass,
Because she will admit no kind of suit, 45
No, not the Duke's.

Viola. There is a fair behavior in thee, Captain,
And though that nature with a beauteous wall
Doth oft close in pollution, yet of thee
I will believe thou hast a mind that suits 50
With this thy fair and outward character.
I prethee (and I'll pay thee bounteously)
Conceal me what I am, and be my aid
For such disguise as haply shall become
The form of my intent. I'll serve this Duke, 55
Thou shalt present me as an eunuch to him;
It may be worth thy pains. For I can sing,
And speak to him in many sorts of music
That will allow me very worth his service.
What else may hap, to time I will commit; 60
Only shape thou thy silence to my wit.

Captain. Be you his eunuch, and your mute I'll be;
When my tongue blabs, then let mine eyes not see.

Viola. I thank thee. Lead me on. *Exeunt.*

SCENE 3

Enter Sir Toby and Maria.

Toby. What a plague means my niece to take the

44 **estate** position in society. **to compass** to achieve. 47 **behavior**
both 'conduct' and 'appearance.' 48 **though** that though. 51 **character** personal appearance. 52 **I prethee** I prithee, I pray thee.
55 **The form of my intent** my outward purpose. 59 **allow me . . .
service** make me very worth while as his servant. 61 **to my wit**
in accordance with my cleverness N. 62 **mute** silent servant (in
contrast with Viola as the sexless servant).

5

death of her brother thus? I am sure care's an enemy
to life.

Maria. By my troth, Sir Toby, you must come in
earlier a nights. Your cousin, my lady, takes great
exceptions to your ill hours. 6

Toby. Why, let her except before excepted.

Maria. Ay, but you must confine yourself within
the modest limits of order. 9

Toby. Confine? I'll confine myself no finer than I
am. These clothes are good enough to drink in, and
so be these boots too. And they be not, let them hang
themselves in their own straps. 13

Maria. That quaffing and drinking will undo you.
I heard my lady talk of it yesterday, and of a foolish
knight that you brought in one night here to be her
wooer.

Toby. Who? Sir Andrew Aguecheek?

Maria. Ay, he.

Toby. He's as tall a man as any's in Illyria. 20

Maria. What's that to th' purpose?

Toby. Why, he has three thousand ducats a year.

Maria. Ay, but he'll have but a year in all these
ducats. He's a very fool and a prodigal. 24

Toby. Fie that you'll say so! He plays o' th' viol-
de-gamboys and speaks three or four languages word

---

4 by my troth truly. 5 a nights of nights. cousin used loosely for
'kinsman,' 'cousin,' 'aunt,' 'nephew,' 'niece.' 7 except before excepted object uselessly to what I do N. 9 modest decent, re-
strained. order good conduct. 10 finer 'tighter' and 'better,' both
of clothing and conduct, with a quibble on 'confine.' 12 be a
regular plural. And if N. 14 undo ruin. 20 tall both 'tall' and
'brave' (ironically of Sir Andrew). 22 ducat an Italian coin N.
24 very true, genuine. 25 viol-de-gamboys 'leg-viola,' predecessor
of the violincello (Italian, *viola da gamba*).

for word without book, and hath all the good gifts
of nature.   28

Maria. He hath indeed, almost natural. For besides
that he's a fool, he's a great quarreler; and but that
he hath the gift of a coward to allay the gust he
hath in quarreling, 'tis thought among the prudent
he would quickly have the gift of a grave.

Toby. By this hand, they are scoundrels and substractors that say so of him. Who are they?   35

Maria. They that add, moreover, he's drunk nightly
in your company.

Toby. With drinking healths to my niece. I'll drink
to her as long as there is a passage in my throat and
drink in Illyria. He's a coward and a coistrel that
will not drink to my niece till his brains turn o'
th' toe like a parish top. What, wench? *Castiliano
vulgo;* for here comes Sir Andrew Agueface.

Enter Sir Andrew.

Andrew. Sir Toby Belch. How now, Sir Toby
Belch?   45

Toby. Sweet Sir Andrew.

Andrew. Bless you, fair shrew.

Maria. And you too, sir.

Toby. Accost, Sir Andrew, accost.

Andrew. What's that?   50

Toby. My niece's chambermaid.

27 **without book** by memory. 29 **almost natural** almost like a
fool N. 31–2 **gust . . . in taste . . .** for. 34 **substractors** detrac-
tors, calumniators. 36 **nightly** 'nightly' and possibly 'knightly,'
'like a knight.' 40 **coistrel** a groom, a base fellow. 42 **parish
top** N. **wench** young girl N. 42–3 **Castiliano vulgo** N. **Agueface**
pale and thin-faced. **Ague** an acute fever, commonly malaria.
46 **sweet** 'dear,' a conventional form of address. 47 **shrew** a
scolding man or woman. 49–55 **Accost . . . Accost** N.

Andrew. Good Mistress Accost, I desire better acquaintance.

Maria. My name is Mary, sir.

Andrew. Good Mistress Mary Accost.　　　　　55

Toby. You mistake, knight. 'Accost' is front her, board her, woo her, assail her.

Andrew. By my troth I would not undertake her in this company. Is that the meaning of 'accost'?

Maria. Fare you well, gentlemen.　　　　　60

Toby. And thou let part so, Sir Andrew, would thou mightst never draw sword agen.

Andrew. And you part so, mistress, I would I might never draw sword agen. Fair lady, do you think you have fools in hand?　　　　　65

Maria. Sir, I have not you by th' hand.

Andrew. Marry, but you shall have, and here's my hand.

Maria. Now, sir, thought is free. I pray you bring your hand to th' butt'ry bar and let it drink.　　　　　70

Andrew. Wherefore, sweetheart? What's your metaphor?

Maria. It's dry, sir.

Andrew. Why, I think so. I am not such an ass but I can keep my hand dry. But what's your jest?　　　　　75

Maria. A dry jest, sir.

52 Andrew F *Ma*[ria]. 55 Mistress Mary Accost F *mistris Mary, accost*. 56 front her face her. 57 **board** 'to greet'; but also 'to go on board,' as of a ship (French, *aborder*). 58 **By my troth** truly. undertake in the literal as well as the figurative sense. 61 **And thou let part so** if you let her go thus. 62 agen again. 63 **And if**. 65 fools in hand fools to do business with. 67 **Marry** originally 'the Virgin Mary,' but here a mild oath, 'indeed,' 'to be sure.' 70 butt'ry bar N. it your hand, i.e. 'Have a drink.' 73 **It's dry, sir** N.

8

Andrew. Are you full of them?

Maria. Ay, sir, I have them at my fingers' ends.
Marry, now I let go your hand, I am barren.   *Exit.*

Toby. O knight, thou lack'st a cup of canary. When
did I see thee so put down?   81

Andrew. Never in your life, I think, unless you see
canary put me down. Methinks sometimes I have no
more wit than a Christian or an ordinary man has.
But I am a great eater of beef and I believe that does
harm to my wit.   86

Toby. No question.

Andrew. And I thought that, I'd forswear it. I'll
ride home tomorrow, Sir Toby.

Toby. *Pourquoi*, my dear knight?   90

Andrew. What is 'pourquoi'? Do, or not do? I
would I had bestowed that time in the tongues that I
have in fencing, dancing, and bear-baiting. O, had
I but followed the arts!   94

Toby. Then hadst thou had an excellent head of
hair.

Andrew. Why, would that have mended my hair?

Toby. Past question, for thou seest it will not curl
by nature.   99

Andrew. But it becomes me well enough, does't not?

Toby. Excellent. It hangs like flax on a distaff;

79 **barren** barren of jokes. 80 **canary** a sweet wine from the
Canary Islands. 81 **put down** discomforted. 83 **methinks** it seems
to me. 83–4 **no more wit than a Christian** no more intelligence
than the average man. 85–6 **great . . . wit** N. wit intellect, mind.
88 **And** if. 90 **Pourquoi** why (French). 93 **bear-baiting** N. 94 **the
arts** liberal learning such as languages. 97 **mended** improved.
98–9 **curl by nature** F *coole my nature.* N. 100 **becomes me** F
becoms we. 101 **like flax on a distaff** like straight strings of flax
on a stick used in spinning.

9

and I hope to see a huswife take thee between her
legs and spin it off.   103

Andrew. Faith, I'll home tomorrow, Sir Toby. Your
niece will not be seen, or if she be, it's four to one
she'll none of me. The Count himself here hard by
woos her.

Toby. She'll none o' th' Count. She'll not match
above her degree, neither in estate, years, nor wit; I
have heard her swear't. Tut, there's life in't, man.

Andrew. I'll stay a month longer. I am a fellow o'
th' strangest mind i' th' world. I delight in masques
and revels sometimes altogether.

Toby. Art thou good at these kick-chawses, knight?

Andrew. As any man in Illyria, whatsoever he be,
under the degree of my betters, and yet I will not
compare with an old man.

Toby. What is thy excellence in a galliard, knight?

Andrew. Faith, I can cut a caper.

Toby. And I can cut the mutton to't.   120

Andrew. And I think I have the back-trick simply
as strong as any man in Illyria.

Toby. Wherefore are these things hid? Wherefore
have these gifts a curtain before 'em? Are they like
to take dust, like Mistress Mall's picture? Why dost
thou not go to church in a galliard and come home
in a coranto? My very walk should be a jig. I would

102 **huswife** housewife, pronounced 'huzzif.' 106 **hard by** near by.
109 **degree** position in society. **estate** fortune. 113 **altogether** in
all respects. 114 **kick-chawses** trifles (French, *quelque chose*). 116
under the degree of my betters except of a social rank higher
than mine. 117 **an old man** probably 'an experienced person.'
118 **galliard** a quick dance in triple time. 119 **caper** ⁊ frolicsome
leap; also a spice used with mutton. 121 **back-trick** a step back-
ward in a dance N. 124 **like** likely. 125 **take** collect. **Mistress
Mall's picture** any woman's portrait N. 127 **coranto** a swift run-
ning dance (French *courante*). **should** would.

not so much as make water but in a sink-a-pace.
What dost thou mean? Is it a world to hide virtues
in? I did think by the excellent constitution of thy
leg, it was form'd under the star of a galliard.   131

Andrew. Ay, 'tis strong, and it does indifferent well
in a dam'd color'd stock. Shall we sit about some
revels?   134

Toby. What shall we do else? Were we not born
under Taurus?

Andrew. Taurus? That's sides and heart.

Toby. No, sir; it is legs and thighs. Let me see thee
caper. Ha, higher; ha, ha, excellent!   *Exeunt.*

SCENE 4

Enter Valentine, and Viola in man's attire.

Valentine. If the Duke continue these favors towards you, Cesario, you are like to be much advanc'd.
He hath known you but three days and already you
are no stranger.   4

Viola. You either fear his humor or my negligence,
that you call in question the continuance of his love.
Is he inconstant, sir, in his favors?

Valentine. No, believe me.

Enter Duke, Curio, and Attendants.

Viola. I thank you. Here comes the Count.

---

128 **sink-a-pace** a rapid dance of five steps (French *cinque-pas*) N.
131 **under the star of a galliard** i.e. under a dancing star. 133
dam'd color'd N. **stock** stocking. **sit** set N. 136 **Taurus** the bull,
one of the signs of the Zodiac N. 137 **That's sides** F *That sides.*
5 **his humor or my negligence** his changeableness or my neglect
(as a servant).

11

Duke. Who saw Cesario, ho?　　　　　　　　　10

Viola. On your attendance, my lord, here.

Duke. Stand you awhile aloof. Cesario,
Thou know'st no less but all. I have unclasp'd
To thee the book even of my secret soul.
Therefore, good youth, address thy gait unto her; 15
Be not denied access, stand at her doors,
And tell them there thy fixed foot shall grow
Till thou have audience.

Viola.　　　　　　　　Sure, my noble lord,
If she be so abandon'd to her sorrow
As it is spoke, she never will admit me.　　　20

Duke. Be clamorous and leap all civil bounds
Rather than make unprofited return.

Viola. Say I do speak with her, my lord, what then?

Duke. O, then unfold the passion of my love;
Surprise her with discourse of my dear faith; 25
It shall become thee well to act my woes.
She will attend it better in thy youth
Than in a nuncio's of more grave aspect.

Viola. I think not so, my lord.

Duke.　　　　　　　　Dear lad, believe it;
For they shall yet belie thy happy years　　30
That say thou art a man. Diana's lip
Is not more smooth and rubious; thy small pipe
Is as the maiden's organ, shrill and sound,

12 **you** all except Cesario. 13 **no less but all** everything. 14 **even** monosyllabic. 15 **address thy gait** direct thy steps. 16 **access** stressed — ´— **doors** N. 21 **clamorous** noisy. **civil** polite. 22 **unprofited** unproductive. 25 **surprise** to overcome suddenly (French *surprendre*). **dear** 'extreme,' commonly used as an intensive. 28 **nuncio's** messenger's. **aspect** stressed — ´—. 32 **rubious** ruby red. **pipe** throat. 33 **sound** clear.

And all is semblative a woman's part.
I know thy constellation is right apt   35
For this affair. Some four or five attend him,
All if you will; for I myself am best
When least in company. Prosper well in this,
And thou shalt live as freely as thy lord
To call his fortunes thine.

    Viola.   I'll do my best   40
To woo your lady: [*Aside.*] yet a barful strife!
Whoe'er I woo, myself would be his wife.   *Exeunt.*

SCENE 5

Enter Maria and Clown.

Maria. Nay, either tell me where thou hast been, **or**
I will not open my lips so wide as a bristle may enter
in way of thy excuse. My lady will hang thee for thy
absence.   4

Clown. Let her hang me. He that is well hang'd in
this world needs to fear no colors.

Maria. Make that good.

Clown. He shall see none to fear.

Maria. A good lenten answer. I can tell thee where
the saying was born, of 'I fear no colors.'   10

Clown. Where, good Mistress Mary?

Maria. In the wars; and that may you be bold to
say in your foolery.

34 **semblative a woman's part** like a woman's actions. a possibly
'of a.' 35 **thy constellation** thy nature N. **apt** suited. 36 **him**
Cesario (on his visit to Olivia). 39 **freely** without restriction.
41 **a barful strife** a conflict full of hindrances. 41–2 **woo . . . woo
. . . would** a verbal quibble N. 6 **to fear no colors** 'to fear nothing,' proverbial N. 9 **lenten** thin, poor.

Clown. Well, God give them wisdom that have it; and those that are fools, let them use their talents. 15

Maria. Yet you will be hang'd for being so long absent, or to be turn'd away. Is not that as good as a hanging to you?

Clown. Many a good hanging prevents a bad marriage; and for turning away, let summer bear it out.

Maria. You are resolute then? 21

Clown. Not so neither; but I am resolv'd on two points.

Maria. That if one break, the other will hold; or if both break, your gaskins fall. 25

Clown. Apt, in good faith; very apt. Well, go thy way. If Sir Toby would leave drinking, thou wert as witty a piece of Eve's flesh as any in Illyria.

Maria. Peace, you rogue; no more o' that. Here comes my lady. Make your excuse wisely, you were best. [*Exit.*] 31

Enter Lady Olivia with Malvolio.

Clown. Wit, and't be thy will, put me into good fooling. Those wits that think they have thee do very oft prove fools; and I that am sure I lack thee may pass for a wise man. For what says Quinapalus? 'Better a witty fool than a foolish wit.' God bless thee, lady.

Olivia. Take the fool away.

14–15 **Well, God . . . talents** N. 20 **for** as for. **away** N. **let summer bear it out** let the warm weather make it (the loss of my job) endurable. 24 **if one [point] break** 'point' in the argument and 'point' as a string used to hold up breeches. 25 **gaskins** loose breeches. 27–8 **If Sir Toby . . . Illyria** N. 30–1 **you were best** it would be best for you. 32 **and't** if it. 35 **Quinapalus** an invention of the Clown.

14

Clown. Do you not hear, fellows? Take away the lady.   40

Olivia. Go to, y'are a dry fool. I'll no more of you. Besides, you grow dishonest.

Clown. Two faults, madonna, that drink and good counsel will amend. For give the dry fool drink, then is the fool not dry. Bid the dishonest man mend himself: if he mend, he is no longer dishonest; if he cannot, let the botcher mend him. Anything that's mended is but patch'd; virtue that transgresses is but patch'd with sin, and sin that amends is but patch'd with virtue. If that this simple syllogism will serve, so; if it will not, what remedy? As there is no true cuckold but calamity, so beauty's a flower. The lady bade take away the fool; therefore I say again, take her away.

Olivia. Sir, I bade them take away you.   55

Clown. Misprision in the highest degree. Lady, *cucullus non facit monachum*. That's as much to say as, I wear not motley in my brain. Good madonna, give me leave to prove you a fool.

Olivia. Can you do it?   60

Clown. Dexteriously, good madonna.

Olivia. Make your proof.

---

41 go to go away, cease. **dry** 'barren,' 'unfruitful,' rather than 'ironical.' **42 dishonest** unreliable (because he has been absent). **43 madonna** my lady (Italian *mia donna*). **44 dry** 'thirsty' and 'barren.' **47 botcher** a mender, especially a tailor or cobbler who does repairs. **47–50 Anything . . . virtue** N. **51–2 As there . . . flower** N. **56–7 Misprision** mistake. **cucullus . . . monachum** the cowl doesn't make the monk. **58 motley** clothing of a mixed color, worn by stage fools N. **61 dexteriously** variant of 'dexterously.'

Clown. I must catechize you for it, madonna. Good
my mouse of virtue, answer me. 64

Olivia. Well, sir, for want of other idleness, I'll bide
your proof.

Clown. Good madonna, why mourn'st thou?

Olivia. Good fool, for my brother's death.

Clown. I think his soul is in hell, madonna.

Olivia. I know his soul is in heaven, fool. 70

Clown. The more fool, madonna, to mourn for your
brother's soul, being in heaven. Take away the fool,
gentlemen.

Olivia. What think you of this fool, Malvolio? Doth
he not mend? 75

Malvolio. Yes, and shall do till the pangs of death
shake him. Infirmity that decays the wise doth ever
make the better fool.

Clown. God send you, sir, a speedy infirmity for the
better increasing your folly. Sir Toby will be sworn
that I am no fox, but he will not pass his word for
twopence that you are no fool.

Olivia. How say you to that, Malvolio? 83

Malvolio. I marvel your ladyship takes delight in
such a barren rascal. I saw him put down the other
day with an ordinary fool that has no more brain
than a stone. Look you now, he's out of his guard
already. Unless you laugh and minister occasion to
him, he is gagg'd. I protest I take these wise men
that crow so at these set kind of fools no better than
the fools' zanies. 91

63–4 **Good my mouse** 'my good mouse'; 'mouse' was a common
term of endearment. **75 mend** get better as to his jokes. **76 shall
do** shall become more foolish. **85–6 barren** empty (of wit), **put
down . . . with** defeated . . . by. **87 out of his guard** without
an answer of wit. **88 minister occasion** give opportunity or open-
ing. **90 set kind** conventional sort. **91 zanies** N.

16

Olivia. O, you are sick of self-love, Malvolio, and taste with a distemper'd appetite. To be generous, guiltless, and of free disposition, is to take those things for bird-bolts that you deem cannon bullets. There is no slander in an allow'd fool, though he do nothing but rail; nor no railing in a known discreet man, though he do nothing but reprove.

Clown. Now Mercury endue thee with leasing, for thou speak'st well of fools.   100

Enter Maria.

Maria. Madam, there is at the gate a young gentleman much desires to speak with you.

Olivia. From the Count Orsino, is it?

Maria. I know not, madam. 'Tis a fair young man and well attended.   105

Olivia. Who of my people hold him in delay?

Maria. Sir Toby, madam, your kinsman.

Olivia. Fetch him off, I pray you. He speaks nothing but madman. Fie on him. [*Exit Maria.*] Go you, Malvolio. If it be a suit from the Count, I am sick or not at home. What you will, to dismiss it. (*Exit Malvolio.*) Now you see, sir, how your fooling grows old and people dislike it.   113

Clown. Thou hast spoke for us, madonna, as if thy eldest son should be a fool; whose scull Jove cram with brains, for here he comes.   116

92 of with. 93 **distemper'd** ill, unhealthy. 95 **bird-bolts** blunt-headed arrows for shooting birds. 96 **no slander in an allow'd fool** N. 99 **Mercury** Mercury was full of guile and tricks. **endue** supply with. **leasing** lying. 109 **madman** like a lunatic. 113 **old** stale. 115 **should be** were going to be (in the future). 116 **he** Sir Toby, drunk.

Enter Sir Toby.

One of thy kin has a most weak *pia mater*.

Olivia. By mine honor, half drunk. What is he at the gate, cousin?

Toby. A gentleman. 120

Olivia. A gentleman? What gentleman?

Toby. 'Tis a gentleman here. A plague o' these pickle-herring! How now, sot?

Clown. Good Sir Toby. 124

Olivia. Cousin, cousin, how have you come so early by this lethargy?

Toby. Lechery, I defy lechery. There's one at the gate.

Olivia. Ay, marry, what is he? 129

Toby. Let him be the divel and he will, I care not. Give me faith, say I. Well, it's all one. *Exit.*

Olivia. What's a drunken man like, fool?

Clown. Like a drown'd man, a fool, and a madman. One draught above heat makes him a fool, the second mads him, and a third drowns him. 135

Olivia. Go, thou, and seek the crowner, and let him sit o' my coz; for he's in the third degree of drink: he's drown'd. Go look after him.

Clown. He is but mad yet, madonna, and the fool shall look to the madman. [*Exit.*]

117 **pia mater** innermost membrane enveloping the brain. 118 **What** 'what' and 'who.' 122 **A plague** N. 123 **sot** fool, clown. 125 **Cousin** loosely for 'kinsman' or 'uncle.' 126 **lethargy** torpor (of drunkenness). 129 **marry** to be sure. 130 **divel** devil. **and** if. 131 **faith** to resist the devil. **it's all one** no difference. 134 **One draught above heat** one drink above the amount to make him normally warm. 136 **crowner** variant of 'coroner.' 137 **sit o' my coz** hold an inquest on my cousin or kinsman (Sir Toby).

Enter Malvolio.

Malvolio. Madam, yond young fellow swears he will speak with you. I told him you were sick; he takes on him to understand so much and therefore comes to speak with you. I told him you were asleep; he seems to have a foreknowledge of that too, and therefore comes to speak with you. What is to be said to him, lady? He's fortified against any denial.

Olivia. Tell him he shall not speak with me.

Malvolio. Has been told so; and he says he'll stand at your door like a sheriff's post and be the supporter to a bench, but he'll speak with you.   151

Olivia. What kind o' man is he?

Malvolio. Why, of mankind.

Olivia. What manner of man?

Malvolio. Of very ill manner. He'll speak with you, will you or no.   156

Olivia. Of what personage and years is he?

Malvolio. Not yet old enough for a man nor young enough for a boy: as a squash is before 'tis a pescod, or a codling when 'tis almost an apple. 'Tis with him in standing water, between boy and man. He is very well favor'd and he speaks very shrewishly. One would think his mother's milk were scarce out of him.

Olivia. Let him approach. Call in my gentlewoman.

Malvolio. Gentlewoman, my lady calls. *Exit.*   165

Enter Maria.

142–3 **on him** upon himself. 149 **Has** he has (from 'h' has'). 150–1 **sheriff's post** . . . **supporter to a bench** N. 159 **squash** unripe pea pod. **pescod** peascod, ripe pea pod. 160 **codling** unripe apple. 161 **standing water** the tide at ebb or flood when it flows neither way. 162 **well favor'd** of good appearance or face. **shrewishly** irritably.

Olivia. Give me my veil; come, throw it o'er my face. We'll once more hear Orsino's embassy.

Enter Viola.

Viola. The honorable lady of the house, which is she? 169

Olivia. Speak to me; I shall answer for her. Your will?

Viola. Most radiant, exquisite, and unmatchable beauty. I pray you tell me if this be the lady of the house, for I never saw her. I would be loath to cast away my speech, for besides that it is excellently well penn'd, I have taken great pains to con it. Good beauties, let me sustain no scorn. I am very comptible, even to the least sinister usage.

Olivia. Whence came you, sir? 179

Viola. I can say little more than I have studied, and that question's out of my part. Good gentle one, give me modest assurance if you be the lady of the house, that I may proceed in my speech.

Olivia. Are you a comedian? 184

Viola. No, my profound heart; and yet (by the very fangs of malice I swear) I am not that I play. Are you the lady of the house?

Olivia. If I do not usurp myself, I am. 188

Viola. Most certain, if you are she, you do usurp yourself; for what is yours to bestow is not yours

167 SD **Enter Viola** F *Enter Violenta* N. (SD is used throughout to indicate stage direction.) 173 **if this be** N. 176 **con** learn, memorize. 177 **sustain** endure, receive (from you). **comptible** spelling variant of 'countable' (sensitive). 178 **the least sinister usage** the least hostile treatment. 182 **modest** moderate. 184 **comedian** actor. 185 **my profound heart** N. 185–6 **the very fangs of malice** the very worst reports and rumors about me. 189–90 **you do usurp yourself** i.e. you should be married.

20

to reserve. But this is from my commission. I will on
with my speech in your praise and then show you
the heart of my message.

Olivia. Come to what is important in't. I forgive
you the praise.   195

Viola. Alas, I took great pains to study it, and 'tis
poetical.

Olivia. It is the more like to be feigned; I pray you
keep it in. I heard you were saucy at my gates, and
allow'd your approach rather to wonder at you than
to hear you. If you be not mad, be gone; if you have
reason, be brief. 'Tis not that time of moon with me
to make one in skipping a dialogue.   203

Maria. Will you hoist sail, sir? Here lies your way.

Viola. No, good swabber; I am to hull here a little
longer. Some mollification for your giant, sweet lady.
Tell me your mind; I am a messenger.

Olivia. Sure you have some hideous matter to deliver, when the courtesy of it is so fearful. Speak
your office.   210

Viola. It alone concerns your ear. I bring no over-
ture of war, no taxation of homage. I hold the olive
in my hand. My words are as full of peace as matter.

Olivia. Yet you began rudely. What are you? What
would you?   215

Viola. The rudeness that hath appear'd in me have
I learn'd from my entertainment. What I am, and

191 **from** in addition to, outside. 194–5 **forgive you** excuse you
(from delivering). 202 **reason** sanity. 202–3 **'Tis not that time
. . . dialogue** N. 204 **Here lies your way** i.e. go. 205 **swabber**
minor officer in charge of cleaning a ship. **to hull** to float without
sail. 206 **giant** (guarding) monster N. 209 **when the courtesy of
it is so fearful** when the manner of delivering it is so frightening.
210 **office** message, business. 212 **taxation of homage** demand or
assessment for submission. 213 **matter** meaning, significance. 214
What are you who are you. 217 **my entertainment** my reception.

what I would, are as secret as maidenhead: to your ears, divinity; to any other's, profanation.

Olivia. Give us the place alone; we will hear this divinity. [*Exit Maria.*] Now, sir, what is your text?

Viola. Most sweet lady.

Olivia. A comfortable doctrine, and much may be said of it. Where lies your text?

Viola. In Orsino's bosom.   225

Olivia. In his bosom? In what chapter of his bosom?

Viola. To answer by the method, in the first of his heart.

Olivia. O, I have read it; it is heresy. Have you no more to say?   230

Viola. Good madam, let me see your face.

Olivia. Have you any commission from your lord to negotiate with my face? You are now out of your text; but we will draw the curtain and show you the picture. [*Unveils.*] Look you, sir, such a one I was this present. Is't not well done?   236

Viola. Excellently done, if God did all.

Olivia. 'Tis in grain, sir; 'twill endure wind and weather.   239

Viola. 'Tis beauty truly blent, whose red and white, Nature's own sweet and cunning hand laid on. Lady, you are the cruel'st she alive If you will lead these graces to the grave, And leave the world no copy.   244

Olivia. O, sir, I will not be so hardhearted. I will

218 **maidenhead** chastity. 219 **divinity** a holy message (of love). 227 **the method** the formal summary of contents. 233–4 **out of your text** off your assigned subject. 236 **this present** a minute ago. 238 **in grain** fast dyed N. 240 **blent** blended. 241 **cunning** skillful.

give out divers schedules of my beauty. It shall be
inventoried and every particle and utensil label'd to
my will: as, item, two lips indifferent red; item, two
grey eyes, with lids to them; item, one neck, one chin,
and so forth. Were you sent hither to praise me?

Viola. I see you what you are; you are too proud;
But if you were the divel, you are fair. 252
My lord and master loves you. O, such love
Could be but recompens'd though you were crown'd
The nonpareil of beauty.

Olivia.   How does he love me? 255

Viola. With adorations, fertill tears,
With groans that thunder love, with sighs of fire.

Olivia. Your lord does know my mind; I cannot love
him.
Yet I suppose him virtuous, know him noble,
Of great estate, of fresh and stainless youth; 260
In voices well divulg'd, free, learn'd, and valiant,
And in dimension and the shape of nature
A gracious person. But yet I cannot love him.
He might have took his answer long ago.

Viola. If I did love you in my master's flame, 265
With such a suff'ring, such a deadly life,
In your denial I would find no sense;
I would not understand it.

Olivia.   Why, what would you?

Viola. Make me a willow cabin at your gate
And call upon my soul within the house; 270

246 **schedules** listings. 247 **utensil** article. **label'd to** added to.
248 **item** namely N. 252 **divel** devil. 256 **fertill tears** fertile tears,
abundant tears. 261 **In voices well divulg'd, free** in public opinion
well reported, generous. 262 **dimension** figure, form of body. 263
gracious graceful. 266 **deadly life** life which is like death. 269
willow a symbol of grief for unrequited love. **cabin** hut.

23

Write loyal cantons of contemned love
And sing them loud even in the dead of night;
Hallow your name to the reverberate hills
And make the babbling gossip of the air
Cry out 'Olivia.' O, you should not rest   275
Between the elements of air and earth
But you should pity me.
   Olivia.   You might do much.
What is your parentage?
   Viola. Above my fortunes, yet my state is well.
I am a gentleman.
   Olivia.   Get you to your lord.   280
I cannot love him. Let him send no more
Unless, perchance, you come to me again
To tell me how he takes it. Fare you well.
I thank you for your pains. Spend this for me.   284
   Viola. I am no fee'd post, lady; keep your purse;
My master, not myself, lacks recompense.
Love make his heart of flint that you shall love;
And let your fervor, like my master's, be
Plac'd in contempt. Farewell, fair cruelty.   *Exit.*
   Olivia. 'What is your parentage?'   290
'Above my fortunes, yet my state is well.
I am a gentleman.' I'll be sworn thou art.
Thy tongue, thy face, thy limbs, actions, and spirit
Do give thee fivefold blazon. Not too fast; soft, soft;
Unless the master were the man. How now?   295

271 **cantons** variant of 'cantos,' 'songs.' **contemned** condemned, rejected. 272 **even** monosyllabic. 273 **Hallow** 'halloa,' 'call out,' and 'make holy.' 274 **babbling gossip** echo. 279 **state** condition, social position. 285 **fee'd post** messenger to be paid or tipped. 287 **Love make** may love make. **that** the antecedent is *his* (of him). 289 **Plac'd in contempt** scorned. 292 **thou art** N. 294 **blazon** a shield or coat of arms in heraldry. 295 **Unless the master were the man** unless Orsino were Cesario.

Even so quickly may one catch the plague?
Methinks I feel this youth's perfections
With an invisible and subtle stealth
To creep in at mine eyes. Well, let it be.
What ho, Malvolio!   300

Enter Malvolio.

Malvolio.   Here, madam, at your service.
Olivia. Run after that same peevish messenger
The County's man. He left this ring behind him,
Would I or not. Tell him I'll none of it.
Desire him not to flatter with his lord   304
Nor hold him up with hopes. I am not for him.
If that the youth will come this way tomorrow,
I'll give him reasons for't. Hie thee, Malvolio.
Malvolio. Madam, I will.   *Exit.*
Olivia. I do I know not what, and fear to find   309
Mine eye too great a flatterer for my mind.
Fate, show thy force: ourselves we do not owe.
What is decreed must be, and be this so.   [*Exit.*]

Finis, Actus primus.

302 County's 'Count's' or 'Duke's'; F *Countes* N. 304 to flatter
with to encourage. 310 **Mine eye . . . mind** N. 311 owe possess,
own, control.

Act II

SCENE 1

Enter Antonio and Sebastian.

Antonio. Will you stay no longer? Nor will you
not that I go with you?

Sebastian. By your patience, no. My stars shine
darkly over me; the malignancy of my fate might
perhaps distemper yours. Therefore I shall crave of
you your leave that I may bear my evils alone. It
were a bad recompense for your love to lay any of
them on you.

Antonio. Let me yet know of you whither you are
bound. 10

Sebastian. No, sooth, sir. My determinate voyage
is mere extravagancy. But I perceive in you so
excellent a touch of modesty that you will not extort from me what I am willing to keep in; therefore it charges me in manners the rather to express
myself. You must know of me then, Antonio, my
name is Sebastian, which I call'd Roderigo. My 17
father was that Sebastian of Messaline whom I
know you have heard of. He left behind him myself
and a sister, both born in an hour. If the heavens

1-2 Nor . . . not N. 3-5 patience allowance, leave. My stars
. . . distemper yours N. 11 sooth truly. determinate determined
upon. 12 extravagancy an extravagant fancy. 13 touch feeling.
15 it charges me in manners I am compelled in good manners.
18 Messaline perhaps Mitylene, but identification is unnecessary.
20 in an hour in the same hour.

26

had been pleas'd, would we had so ended. But you,
sir, alter'd that, for some hour before you took me
from the breach of the sea was my sister drown'd.

Antonio. Alas the day!   24

Sebastian. A lady, sir, though it was said she much
resembled me, was yet of many accounted beautiful.
But though I could not with such estimable wonder
overfar believe that, yet thus far I will boldly publish her: she bore a mind that envy could not but
call fair. She is drown'd already, sir, with salt
water, though I seem to drown her remembrance
again with more.   32

Antonio. Pardon me, sir, your bad entertainment.

Sebastian. O good Antonio, forgive me your trouble.

Antonio. If you will not murther me for my love,
let me be your servant.   36

Sebastian. If you will not undo what you have done,
that is, kill him whom you have recover'd, desire it
not. Fare ye well at once. My bosom is full of kindness; and I am yet so near the manners of my
mother that, upon the least occasion more, mine
eyes will tell tales of me. I am bound to the Count
Orsino's court. Farewell.   *Exit.*   43

Antonio. The gentleness of all the gods go with
    thee.

I have many enemies in Orsino's court,   45
Else would I very shortly see thee there.

23 the breach of the sea the breaking waves, usually on a coast.
27 with such estimable wonder with so much admiring wonder
(for her). 28 publish declare, describe publicly. 33 your bad entertainment the poor hospitality I have given you. 34 your trouble
for causing you trouble. 35 murther me for my love i.e. kill me
by leaving me. for in reward for. 38 recover'd saved. 44 gentleness
kindliness.

But come what may, I do adore thee so
That danger shall seem sport and I will go.   *Exit.*

SCENE 2

Enter Viola and Malvolio at several doors.

Malvolio. Were not you ev'n now with the Countess
Olivia?

Viola. Even now, sir. On a moderate pace I have
since arriv'd but hither.   4

Malvolio. She returns this ring to you, sir. You
might have saved me my pains to have taken it
away yourself. She adds, moreover, that you should
put your lord into a desperate assurance she will
none of him. And one thing more, that you be never
so hardy to come again in his affairs, unless it be
to report your lord's taking of this. Receive it so.

Viola. She took the ring of me. I'll none of it.   12

Malvolio. Come, sir, you peevishly threw it to her;
and her will is, it should be so return'd. If it be
worth stooping for, there it lies, in your eye; if not,
be it his that finds it.   *Exit.*

Viola. I left no ring with her. What means this
      lady?   17
Fortune forbid my outside have not charmed her.
She made good view of me; indeed, so much

SD Enter . . . at several doors N. 3 On a moderate pace at a
moderate walking pace. 6 to have taken it if you had taken it.
8 a desperate assurance she will none of him an extreme assurance leaving no hope that she will have any part of him. 10 so
hardy to come so venturesome as to come. 18 not emphatic negative attached to *forbid.* 19 made good view of me looked favor-
ably at me.

That methought her eyes had lost her tongue,   20
For she did speak in starts distractedly.
She loves me sure; the cunning of her passion
Invites me in this churlish messenger.
None of my lord's ring? Why, he sent her none.
I am the man. If it be so, as 'tis,   25
Poor lady, she were better love a dream.
Disguise, I see thou art a wickedness
Wherein the pregnant enemy does much.
How easy is it for the proper false
In women's waxen hearts to set their forms.   30
Alas, O, frailty is the cause, not we,
For such as we are made, if such we be.
How will this fadge? My master loves her dearly;
And I (poor monster) fond as much on him;
And she (mistaken) seems to dote on me.   35
What will become of this? As I am man,
My state is desperate for my master's love.
As I am woman (now alas the day!),
What thriftless sighs shall poor Olivia breathe?
O Time, thou must untangle this, not I;   40
It is too hard a knot for me t' untie.   [*Exit.*]

SCENE 3

Enter Sir Toby and Sir Andrew.

Toby. Approach, Sir Andrew. Not to be abed after

20 methought it seemed to me. her eyes had lost her tongue
what she saw had caused her to lose her tongue. 22 cunning
craftiness. 23 in through. 28 pregnant enemy strong enemy N.
29 the proper false i.e. those who appear to be respectable and
genuine but are deceivers. 30 forms 'impressions' as of a seal,
and 'appearance.' 31-2 Alas . . . such we be N. 33 fadge fit, be
suitable. 34 monster because of both sexes. fond dote. 37 desperate pronounced 'desp'rate.' 39 thriftless unprofitable.

midnight is to be up betimes, and *diluculo surgere*,
thou know'st.

Andrew. Nay, by my troth, I know not; but I know
to be up late is to be up late. 5

Toby. A false conclusion; I hate it as an unfill'd
can. To be up after midnight and to go to bed then,
is early; so that to go to bed after midnight is to go
to bed betimes. Does not our lives consist of the
four elements? 10

Andrew. Faith, so they say; but I think it rather
consists of eating and drinking.

Toby. Th' art a scholar. Let us therefore eat and
drink. Marian, I say, a stoup of wine.

Enter Clown.

Andrew. Here comes the fool, i' faith. 15

Clown. How now, my hearts? Did you never see the
picture of We Three?

Toby. Welcome, ass. Now let's have a catch. 18

Andrew. By my troth, the fool has an excellent
breast. I had rather than forty shillings I had such
a leg and so sweet a breath to sing as the fool has.
In sooth, thou wast in very gracious fooling last
night when thou spok'st of Pigrogromitus, of the
Vapians passing the equinoctial of Queubus. 'Twas
very good, i' faith. I sent thee sixpence for thy
leman. Hadst it? 26

2 betimes early. diluculo surgere to get up at dawn; F *Deliculo* N.
4 by my troth truly. 7 can metal vessel for holding liquor. 9–10
Does not . . . elements N. 14 stoup a drinking vessel. 16 hearts
a term of endearment. 17 the picture of We Three N. 18 a catch
a musical round in which one singer 'catches' at the words of
another. 20 breast lungs, hence voice in singing. 22 gracious
graceful, elegant. 23–4 Pigrogomitus . . . Queubus the names
are meaningless. 26 leman sweetheart.

Clown. I did impeticos thy gratillity, for Malvolio's nose is no whipstock. My lady has a white hand, and the Myrmidons are no bottle-ale houses. 29

Andrew. Excellent. Why, this is the best fooling, when all is done. Now a song.

Toby. Come on, there is sixpence for you. Let's have a song.

Andrew. There's a testril of me too. If one knight give a ——— 35

Clown. Would you have a love song, or a song of good life?

Toby. A love song, a love song.

Andrew. Ay, ay. I care not for good life.

Clown sings.

> O mistress mine, where are you roaming? 40
> O, stay and hear, your true love's coming,
> That can sing both high and low.
> Trip no further, pretty sweeting;
> Journeys end in lovers meeting,
> Every wise man's son doth know. 45

Andrew. Excellent good, i' faith.
Toby. Good, good.

Clown [sings].

> What is love? 'Tis not hereafter;
> Present mirth hath present laughter;
> What's to come is still unsure. 50
> In delay there lies no plenty;
> Then come kiss me, sweet and twenty:
> Youth's a stuff will not endure.

27–9 I did impeticos thy gratillity . . . bottle-ale houses N. 34 testril diminutive of 'tester,' 'sixpence.' of from. 35 give a ——— F *give a.* 37 good life virtuous living. 40 O mistress mine N. 50 still always. 52 sweet and twenty 'sweet and twenty times sweet' or 'sweet and twenty years old.'

Andrew. A mellifluous voice, as I am true knight.

Toby. A contagious breath. 55

Andrew. Very sweet and contagious, i' faith.

Toby. To hear by the nose, it is dulcet in contagion. But shall we make the welkin dance indeed? Shall we rouse the night owl in a catch that will draw three souls out of one weaver? Shall we do that? 60

Andrew. And you love me, let's do't. I am dog at a catch.

Clown. By'r Lady, sir, and some dogs will catch well. 64

Andrew. Most certain. Let our catch be 'Thou knave.'

Clown. 'Hold thy peace, thou knave,' knight? I shall be constrain'd in't to call thee knave, knight.

Andrew. 'Tis not the first time I have constrained one to call me knave. Begin, fool. It begins, 'Hold thy peace.' 71

Clown. I shall never begin if I hold my peace.

Andrew. Good, i' faith; come, begin.

Catch sung. Enter Maria.

Maria. What a caterwauling do you keep here? If my lady have not call'd up her steward Malvolio and bid him turn you out of doors, never trust me. 76

Toby. My lady's a Catayan, we are politicians, Malvolio's a Peg-a-Ramsey, and [*Sings.*] 'Three

55 **A contagious breath** 'a catchy voice or tune,' also 'a bad breath.' 57 **To hear . . . contagion** N. 58 **the welkin** the sky. 59 **a catch** a round (of singing). 59–60 **draw three souls out of one weaver** N. 61 **and** if. 61–62 **I am dog at a catch** I am an expert at a round (of singing). 63 **By'r Lady** 'by our Lady' (the Virgin Mary), a petty oath. 65–6 **'Thou knave'** N. 74 **caterwauling** the cry of the cat at rutting time. 77 **Catayan** person of no account, scoundrel N. **politicians** statesmen concerned with important questions. 78 **a Peg-a-Ramsey** probably 'a lewd, coarse person' N.

merry men be we.' Am not I consanguineous? Am I not of her blood? Tilly vally, lady [*Sings.*], 'There dwelt a man in Babylon, lady, lady.' 81

Clown. Beshrew me, the knight's in admirable fooling.

Andrew. Ay, he does well enough if he be dispos'd, and so do I too. He does it with a better grace, but I do it more natural. 86

Toby. [*Sings.*] 'O the twelfe day of December.'

Maria. For the love o' God, peace.

Enter Malvolio.

Malvolio. My masters, are you mad? Or what are you? Have you no wit, manners, nor honesty, but to gabble like tinkers at this time of night? Do ye make an alehouse of my lady's house, that ye squeak out your coziers' catches without any mitigation or remorse of voice? Is there no respect of place, persons, nor time in you? 95

Toby. We did keep time, sir, in our catches. Sneck up.

Malvolio. Sir Toby, I must be round with you. My lady bade me tell you that though she harbors you as her kinsman, she's nothing allied to your disorders. If you can separate yourself and your misdemeanors, you are welcome to the house. If not,

78–9 'Three merry men be we' N. consanguineous related. 86 Tilly vally nonsense. 80–1 'There dwelt a man' N. 82 Beshrew me 'curse me,' a mild oath. 86 natural 'naturally,' but also 'a fool,' 'like a fool.' 87 'O the twelfe day of December' N. twelfe twelfth. 90 wit sense. honesty respectability. 93 coziers' catches cobblers' musical rounds. 93–4 mitigation or remorse lessening or regret. 94 respect of respect for. 96–7 Sneck up snick up, go hang. 98 round plain.

and it would please you to take leave of her, she is
very willing to bid you farewell.   104

Toby. [*Sings.*] 'Farewell, dear heart, since I must
needs be gone.'

Maria. Nay, good Sir Toby.

Clown. [*Sings.*] 'His eyes do show his days are
almost done.'

Malvolio. Is't even so?   110

Toby. [*Sings.*] 'But I will never die.'

Clown. Sir Toby, there you lie.

Malvolio. This is much credit to you.

Toby. [*Sings.*] 'Shall I bid him go?'

Clown. [*Sings.*] 'What and if you do?'   115

Toby. [*Sings.*] 'Shall I bid him go, and spare not?'

Clown. [*Sings.*] 'O, no, no, no, no, you dare not.'

Toby. Out o' tune, sir? Ye lie. Art any more than
a steward? Dost thou think because thou art virtu-
ous, there shall be no more cakes and ale?   120

Clown. Yes, by St. Anne, and ginger shall be hot
i' th' mouth too.

Toby. Th' art i' th' right. Go, sir, rub your chain
with crumbs. A stoup of wine, Maria.   124

Malvolio. Mistress Mary, if you priz'd my lady's
favor at anything more than contempt, you would
not give means for this uncivil rule. She shall know
of it, by this hand.   *Exit.*

Maria. Go shake your ears.   129

Andrew. 'Twere as good a deed as to drink when a

103 and if. 105 'Farewell, dear heart' N. 112 there you lie i.e. you
are a liar. 115 and if if. 120 cakes and ale N. 121 St. Anne N.
ginger N. 123–4 rub your chain with crumbs N. 124 a stoup a
cup. 127 give means i.e. bring the wine. uncivil rule disorderly
revel. 128 by this hand a mild exclamation. 129 Go shake
your ears i.e. you are an ass. 130 as good a deed as to drink N.

man's ahungry, to challenge him the field and then
to break promise with him and make a fool of him.

Toby. Do't, knight. I'll write thee a challenge; or
I'il deliver thy indignation to him by word of mouth.

Maria. Sweet Sir Toby, be patient for tonight.
Since the youth of the Count's was today with my
lady, she is much out of quiet. For Monsieur Malvolio, let me alone with him. If I do not gull him into
a nayword and make him a common recreation, do
not think I have wit enough to lie straight in my bed.
I know I can do it.   141

Toby. Possess us, possess us. Tell us something of
him.

Maria. Marry, sir, sometimes he is a kind of Puritan.   145

Andrew. O, if I thought that, I'd beat him like a
dog.

Toby. What, for being a Puritan? Thy exquisite
reason, dear knight.   149

Andrew. I have no exquisite reason for't, but I have
reason good enough.

Maria. The div'l a Puritan that he is, or anything
constantly but a time-pleaser, an affection'd ass, that
cons state without book and utters it by great
swarths. The best persuaded of himself, so cramm'd
(as he thinks) with excellencies that it is his grounds

131 **to challenge him the field** to challenge him to the field of
battle. 135 **Sweet** dear. 138 **gull** trick. 139 **a nayword** a byword;
F *an ayword.* 139 **recreation** 'pastime' or 'amusement.' 142 **Possess us** give us the facts. 144 **Marry** indeed. **a kind of Puritan** N.
152 **div'l** devil. 153 **a time-pleaser** a sycophant, a toady. **affection'd** affected. 154 **cons state without book** studies and learns a
stately manner by heart. 155 **swarths** quantities N. **The best
persuaded of himself** the highest opinion of himself. 156–7
grounds of faith firm belief.

of faith that all that look on him love him; and on
that vice in him will my revenge find notable cause to
work.

Toby. What wilt thou do? 160

Maria. I will drop in his way some obscure epistles
of love wherein by the color of his beard, the shape
of his leg, the manner of his gait, the expressure of
his eye, forehead, and complexion, he shall find himself most feelingly personated. I can write very like
my lady your niece; on a forgotten matter we can
hardly make distinction of our hands.

Toby. Excellent. I smell a device.

Andrew. I have't in my nose too. 169

Toby. He shall think by the letters that thou wilt
drop that they come from my niece, and that she's
in love with him.

Maria. My purpose is indeed a horse of that color.

Andrew. And your horse now would make him an
ass. 175

Maria. Ass, I doubt not.

Andrew. O, 'twill be admirable.

Maria. Sport royal, I warrant you. I know my
physic will work with him. I will plant you two and
let the fool make a third, where he shall find the
letter. Observe his construction of it. For this night,
to bed and dream on the event. Farewell.   *Exit.*

Toby. Good night, Penthesilea.

Andrew. Before me, she's a good wench. 184

163 expressure expression. 165 personated represented. 167 distinction of our hands difference in our handwritings. 176 Ass both
'ass' and 'as.' 179 physic 'medicine' in the sense of 'cure' for
Malvolio's conceit. 180 let the fool make a third N. he Malvolio.
181 construction interpretation. 182 the event the outcome. 183
Penthesilea Queen of the Amazons (ironically). 184 Before me
I swear by myself.

Toby. She's a beagle true bred, and one that adores me. What o' that?

Andrew. I was ador'd once too.

Toby. Let's to bed, knight. Thou hadst need send for more money. 189

Andrew. If I cannot recover your niece, I am a foul way out.

Toby. Send for money, knight. If thou hast her not i' th' end, call me Cut.

Andrew. If I do not, never trust me, take it how you will. 195

Toby. Come, come; I'll go burn some sack. 'Tis too late to go to bed now. Come, knight; come, knight.

Exeunt.

SCENE 4

Enter Duke, Viola, Curio, and others.

Duke. Give me some music. Now good morrow, friends.
Now, good Cesario, but that piece of song,
That old and anticke song we heard last night.
Methought it did relieve my passion much,
More than light airs and recollected terms 5
Of these most brisk and giddy-paced times.
Come, but one verse.

Curio. He is not here, so please your lordship, that should sing it.

185 a beagle a small rabbit hound. 190 **recover** 'win,' 'gain,' possibly with the legal force of 'gain title to.' 190–1 **a foul way out** miserably out of money. 193 **Cut** a horse with a short tail. 196 **burn some sack** warm some sherry. 1 **morrow** morning. 3 **anticke** antique, old-fashioned (stressed `⌣ —`). 5 **recollected** studied, learned.

Duke. Who was it? 10

Curio. Feste the jester, my lord, a fool that the Lady Olivia's father took much delight in. He is about the house.

Duke. Seek him out, and play the tune the while.

[*Exit Curio.*] *Music plays.*

Come hither, boy. If ever thou shalt love, 15
In the sweet pangs of it remember me;
For such as I am, all true lovers are,
Unstaid and skittish in all motions else
Save in the constant image of the creature
That is belov'd. How dost thou like this tune? 20

Viola. It gives a very echo to the seat
Where love is thron'd.

Duke.   Thou dost speak masterly.
My life upon't, young though thou art, thine eye
Hath stay'd upon some favor that it loves.
Hath it not, boy?

Viola.   A little, by your favor. 25

Duke. What kind of woman is't?

Viola.   Of your complexion.

Duke. She is not worth thee then. What years, i'
faith?

Viola. About your years, my lord.

Duke. Too old, by heaven. Let still the woman take
An elder than herself; so wears she to him, 30
So sways she level in her husband's heart.
For, boy, however we do praise ourselves,

---

18 **in all motions else** in all other emotions or feelings. 21 **the seat** the heart. 22 **masterly** in an experienced manner. 24 **favor** 'face'; in l. 25 Viola puns on 'favor.' 29 **still** always. 30 **so wears she to him** so she adapts herself to him. 31 **so sways she level** so she keeps constant her husband's love.

Our fancies are more giddy and unfirm,
More longing, wavering, sooner lost and worn. 34
Than women's are.

 Viola.   I think it well, my Lord.

 Duke. Then let thy love be younger than thyself,
Or thy affection cannot hold the bent;
For women are as roses whose fair flow'r,
Being once display'd, doth fall that very hour.

 Viola. And so they are; alas, that they are so. 40
To die, even when they to perfection grow.

Enter Curio and Clown.

 Duke. O fellow, come, the song we had last night.
Mark it, Cesario; it is old and plain.
The spinsters and the knitters in the sun,
And the free maids that weave their thread with
  bones, 45
Do use to chant it. It is silly sooth,
And dallies with the innocence of love
Like the old age.

 Clown. Are you ready, sir? 49

 Duke. I prethee sing.   *Music.*

The Song.

 Come away, come away, death,
 And in sad cypress let me be laid.

---

33 **Our fancies** men's loves. 34 **worn** worn out N. 37 **hold the bent**
'keep the intensity,' as in a bent bow; or 'hold the direction.'
41 **even** monosyllabic. 44 **spinsters** spinners. 45 **free** happy, care-
free. **weave their thread with bones** make bone or thread lace
with bone bobbins. 46 **do use to** are accustomed to. **silly sooth**
simple truth. 47 **dallies with** treats lightly of. 48 **the old age** the
former times (of virtue). 50 **I prethee** I pray thee. 51 **Come away**
'come away from there,' i.e. 'come here.' 52 **cypress** a coffin of
cypress wood, boughs of cypress, or thin black cloth (all associated with mourning).

Fie, away; fie, away, breath;
I am slain by a fair cruel maid.
  My shroud of white, stuck all with yew, **55**
    O, prepare it.
  My part of death, no one so true
    Did share it.

Not a flower, not a flower sweet
On my black coffin let there be strown. **60**
Not a friend, not a friend greet
My poor corpse, where my bones shall be thrown.
  A thousand thousand sighs to save,
    Lay me, O, where
  Sad true lover never find my grave, **65**
    To weep there.

Duke. There's for thy pains.

Clown. No pains, sir. I take pleasure in singing, sir.

Duke. I'll pay thy pleasure then. **69**

Clown. Truly, sir, and pleasure will be paid one time or another.

Duke. Give me now leave to leave thee. **72**

Clown. Now the melancholy god protect thee, and the tailor make thy doublet of changeable taffeta, for thy mind is a very opal. I would have men of such constancy put to sea, that their business might be everything, and their intent everywhere; for that's it that always makes a good voyage of nothing. Farewell. *Exit.*

53 **Fie, away** fie, go away N. 55 **yew** the yew tree, associated with mourning. 57–8 **My part . . . share it** N. 70 **pleasure will be paid** indulgence exacts its penalty N. 73 the **melancholy god** N. 74 **doublet** a closely fitted jacket. **taffeta** a thin silk cloth. 75 **opal** a semiprecious stone of changeable color. 75–8 **I would have . . . voyage of nothing** N.

Duke. Let all the rest give place.

                        [Exeunt Curio and Attendants.]

                            Once more, Ce-

sario,   80

Get thee to yond same sovereign cruelty.

Tell her my love, more noble than the world,

Prizes not quantity of dirty lands.

The parts that fortune hath bestow'd upon her,

Tell her I hold as giddily as fortune.   85

But 'tis that miracle and queen of gems

That nature pranks her in, attracts my soul.

  Viola. But if she cannot love you, sir.

  Duke. I cannot be so answer'd.

  Viola.   Sooth, but you must.

Say that some lady, as perhaps there is,   90

Hath for your love as great a pang of heart

As you have for Olivia. You cannot love her.

You tell her so. Must she not then be answer'd?

  Duke. There is no woman's sides

Can bide the beating of so strong a passion   95

As love doth give my heart; no woman's heart

So big to hold so much; they lack retention.

Alas, their love may be call'd appetite,

No motion of the liver, but the palate

That suffer surfeit, cloyment, and revolt.   100

But mine is all as hungry as the sea

And can digest as much; make no compare

---

80 **give place** leave. 81 **sovereign cruelty** supremely cruel person
(Olivia). 83 **dirty** 'made of earth or dirt' and 'filthy.' 84 **parts**
possessions, attributes. **fortune** luck, chance. 85 **giddily** lightly.
87 **pranks her in** decks her or dresses her in. 89 **I cannot** F *It
cannot* N. 89 **Sooth** truly. 94–5 **woman's sides Can bide** N. **bide**
withstand, endure. 97 **they lack retention** women lack the capacity of retaining. 99–100 **No motion . . . and revolt.** N.

Between that love a woman can bear me
And that I owe Olivia.

Viola.　　　　　　Ay, but I know.

Duke. What dost thou know?　　　　　　105

Viola. Too well what love women to men may owe.
In faith, they are as true of heart as we.
My father had a daughter lov'd a man
As it might be perhaps, were I a woman,
I should your lordship.

Duke.　　　　　　And what's her history?　　110

Viola. A blank, my lord. She never told her love,
But let concealment like a worm i' th' bud,
Feed on her damask cheek. She pin'd in thought;
And with a green and yellow melancholy,
She sat like Patience on a monument,　　　　　　115
Smiling at grief. Was not this love indeed?
We men may say more, swear more; but indeed
Our shows are more than will; for still we prove
Much in our vows, but little in our love.

Duke. But died thy sister of her love, my boy?　　120

Viola. I am all the daughters of my father's house,
And all the brothers too; and yet I know not.
Sir, shall I to this lady?

Duke.　　　　　　Ay, that's the theme.
To her in haste. Give her this jewel. Say　　　　　　124
My love can give no place, bide no denay.　　　*Exeunt.*

104 owe have toward; so also l. 106. 113 damask of variegated
color, here pink and white as of a damask rose. 114–16 And with
. . . smiling at grief N. 118 Our shows . . . will N. still always.
125 can give no place cannot yield. denay denial.

SCENE 5

Enter Sir Toby, Sir Andrew, and Fabian.

Toby. Come thy ways, Signior Fabian.

Fabian. Nay, I'll come. If I lose a scruple of this sport, let me be boil'd to death with melancholy.

Toby. Wouldst thou not be glad to have the niggardly rascally sheep-biter come by some notable shame?   6

Fabian. I would exult, man. You know he brought me out o' favor with my lady about a bear-baiting here.   9

Toby. To anger him we'll have the bear again; and we will fool him black and blue, shall we not, Sir Andrew?

Andrew. And we do not, it is pity of our lives.

Enter Maria.

Toby. Here comes the little villain. How now, my metal of India?   15

Maria. Get ye all three into the box tree. Malvolio's coming down this walk. He has been yonder i' the sun practicing behavior to his own shadow this half hour. Observe him, for the love of mockery; for I know this letter will make a contemplative idiot of him. Close, in the name of jesting. [*The others hide.*]

1 Come thy ways come along on your way. 2 a scruple a bit N. 3 let me . . . melancholy N. 5 sheep-biter a dog that bites sheep, a sneaking fellow. 7–9 You know . . . a bear-baiting here N. 13 And if. 14–15 my metal of India my golden one N. 18 behavior elegant conduct. 20–1 make a contemplative idiot of him fill him with idiotic thoughts 21 close hide.

Lie thou there, [*Throws down a letter.*] for here comes the trout that must be caught with tickling.

Exit.

Enter Malvolio.

Malvolio. 'Tis but fortune, all is fortune. Maria once told me she did affect me; and I have heard herself come thus near, that should she fancy, it should be one of my complexion. Besides, she uses me with a more exalted respect than anyone else that follows her. What should I think on't?

Toby. Here's an overweening rogue.   30

Fabian. O, peace! Contemplation makes a rare turkey cock of him. How he jets under his advanc'd plumes!

Andrew. 'Slight, I could so beat the rogue.

Toby. Peace, I say.   35

Malvolio. To be Count Malvolio.

Toby. Ah, rogue!

Andrew. Pistol him, pistol him.

Toby. Peace, peace.   39

Malvolio. There is example for't. The Lady of the Strachy married the yeoman of the wardrobe.

Andrew. Fie on him, Jezebel.

Fabian. O, peace! Now he's deeply in. Look how imagination blows him.   44

23 trout . . . tickling N. 25 she did affect me Olivia was inclined to love me. 27 complexion personality, temperament N. 28–9 follows her is in her service. 32–3 jets under his advanc'd plumes struts under his stiffened feathers. 34 'Slight 'by God's light,' a mild oath. 35 Toby N. 38 Pistol him shoot him. 40–1 The Lady of the Strachy N. 41 the yeoman of the wardrobe the servant in charge of the clothing and linen of a noble family. 42 Fie on him, Jezebel N. 44 blows him puffs him up.

Malvolio. Having been three months married to her, sitting in my state.

Toby. O, for a stonebow to hit him in the eye!

Malvolio. Calling my officers about me, in **my** branch'd velvet gown; having come from a day bed, where I have left Olivia sleeping.   50

Toby. Fire and brimstone!

Fabian. O, peace, peace!

Malvolio. And then to have the humor of state; and after a demure travel of regard—telling them I know my place, as I would they should do theirs—to ask for my kinsman Toby.   56

Toby. Bolts and shackles!

Fabian. O, peace, peace, peace, now, now!

Malvolio. Seven of my people with an obedient start make out for him. I frown the while, and perchance wind up my watch, or play with my— some rich jewel. Toby approaches; curtsies there to me.

Toby. Shall this fellow live?

Fabian. Though our silence be drawn from us with cars, yet peace.   65

Malvolio. I extend my hand to him thus, quenching my familiar smile with an austere regard of control.

Toby. And does not Toby take you a blow o' the lips then?   69

Malvolio. Saying, 'Cousin Toby, my fortunes hav-

---

46 **state** dignity, seat of state. 47 **a stonebow** a crossbow or catapult for shooting stones. 49 **branch'd** embroidered with figures of branches or flowers. **a day bed** a couch. 53 **the humor of state** the manner and disposition of authority. 54 **a demure travel of regard** a grave survey of observation N. 56 **my kinsman Toby** Malvolio omits the title 'Sir.' 60 **make out** go out. 61 **my— some rich** F *my some rich* N. 64-5 **with cars** by force, by terrible violence N. 67 **control** authority. 68 **take you** give you.

ing cast me on your niece, give me this prerogative of speech.'

Toby. What, what?

Malvolio. 'You must amend your drunkenness.'

Toby. Out, scab.   75

Fabian. Nay, patience, or we break the sinews of our plot.

Malvolio. 'Besides, you waste the treasure of your time with a foolish knight.'

Andrew. That's me, I warrant you.   80

Malvolio. 'One Sir Andrew.'

Andrew. I knew 'twas I, for many do call me fool.

Malvolio. What employment have we here?

[*Takes up the letter.*]

Fabian. Now is the woodcock near the gin.   84

Toby. O, peace, and the spirit of humors intimate reading aloud to him.

Malvolio. By my life, this is my lady's hand. These be her very C's, her U's, and her T's, and thus makes she her great P's. It is in contempt of question her hand.   90

Andrew. Her C's, her U's, and her T's; why that?

Malvolio. [*Reads.*] 'To the unknown belov'd, this, and my good wishes.' Her very phrases. By your leave, wax. Soft. And the impressure her Lucrece, with which she uses to seal. 'Tis my lady. To whom should this be?   96

Fabian. This wins him, liver and all.

75 Out, scab away, scurvy fellow. 83 **employment** affair, matter. 84 **woodcock . . . gin** N. gin snare, trap. 85–6 **the spirit . . . to him** N. 88–9 **her very C's . . . P's** N. 89 **in contempt of question** beyond question. 93–4 **By your leave, wax** N. 94 **Soft** careful, slow. **Lucrece** N. 95 **uses** is accustomed to. 97 **liver** the seat of passion.

Malvolio. [*Reads.*]

> Jove knows I love,
> But who?
> Lips, do not move,
> No man must know.   **100**

'No man must know.' What follows? The numbers
alter'd. 'No man must know.' If this should be thee,
Malvolio?

Toby. Marry, hang thee, brock.   **105**

Malvolio. [*Reads.*]

> I may command where I adore,
> But silence like a Lucrece knife,
> With bloodless stroke my heart doth gore.
> M. O. A. I. doth sway my life.

Fabian. A fustian riddle.   **110**

Toby. Excellent wench, say I.

Malvolio. 'M. O. A. I. doth sway my life.' Nay, but
first let me see, let me see, let me see.

Fabian. What dish o' poison has she dress'd him!

Toby. And with what wing the staniel checks at it!

Malvolio. 'I may command where I adore.' Why, she
may command me: I serve her; she is my lady. Why,
this is evident to any formal capacity. There is no
obstruction in this. And the end; what should that
alphabetical position portend? If I could make that
resemble something in me? Softly. 'M. O. A. I.'   **121**

102–3 **The numbers alter'd** the meters or accents of verse altered
N. 105 **brock** badger N. 110 **fustian** ridiculously lofty N. 111
Excellent wench clever girl (of Maria). 114 **What** what a. **dress'd**
prepared. 115 **And with . . . at it** N. **staniel** an inferior hawk;
F *Stallion.* 118 **formal capacity** normal intellect. 119 **obstruction**
difficulty. 119 **what should** what would. 120 **position** order. 121
Softly easily, carefully.

Toby. O, ay, make up that. He is now at a cold scent.

Fabian. Sowter will cry upon't for all this, though it be as rank as a fox. 125

Malvolio. M., Malvolio, M. Why, that begins my name.

Fabian. Did not I say he would work it out? The cur is excellent at faults. 129

Malvolio. M. But then there is no consonancy in the sequel. That suffers under probation. A should follow, but O does.

Fabian. And O shall end, I hope.

Toby. Ay, or I'll cudgel him and make him cry O.

Malvolio. And then I comes behind. 135

Fabian. Ay, and you had any eye behind you, you might see more detraction at your heels than fortunes before you.

Malvolio. 'M. O. A. I.' This simulation is not as the former; and yet to crush this a little, it would bow to me, for every one of these letters are in my name. Soft, here follows prose. 142

[*Reads.*] 'If this fall into thy hand, revolve. In my stars I am above thee, but be not afraid of greatness. Some are born great, some achieve greatness, and some have greatness thrust upon 'em. Thy fates open their hands; let thy blood and spirit embrace them;

122 Make up that put that together. 122–3 a cold scent an old and difficult trail, a false trail. 124–5 Sowter . . . fox N. 129 faults gaps or breaks in the scent N. 130–1 But then . . . probation N. 133 And O shall end N. 136 And if. any eye behind you N. 137 more detraction at your heels more loss of face and humiliation coming directly after you. 139 simulation puzzle, hidden meaning. 140–1 and yet . . . bow to me N. 142 Soft carefully, slowly. 143 revolve think, consider. 144 my stars my fate, my position. 145 born F *become.* achieve F *atcheeves* N.

48

and to inure thyself to what thou art like to be, cast
thy humble slough and appear fresh. Be opposite
with a kinsman, surly with servants. Let thy tongue
tang arguments of state. Put thyself into the trick
of singularity. She thus advises thee that sighs for
thee. Remember who commended thy yellow stockings
and wish'd to see thee ever cross-garter'd. I say remember; go to; thou art made if thou desir'st to be
so. If not, let me see thee a steward still, the fellow
of servants, and not worthy to touch Fortune's fingers. Farewell. She that would alter services with
thee,   159
            'The Fortunate-Unhappy.'
Daylight and champian discovers not more. This is
open, I will be proud, I will read politic authors, I
will baffle Sir Toby, I will wash off gross acquaintance, I will be point devise, the very man. I do not
now fool myself to let imagination jade me; for
every reason excites to this, that my lady loves me.
She did commend my yellow stockings of late; she
did praise my leg being cross-garter'd; and in this
she manifests herself to my love, and with a kind of
injunction drives me to these habits of her liking.
I thank my stars, I am happy. I will be strange,
stout, in yellow stockings and cross-garter'd, even

148 **inure** get used to. **like** likely. 148–9 **cast . . . fresh** N. 151
tang sound with, echo with N. 152 **singularity** eccentricity. 154
cross-garter'd N. 155 **go to** go on. 158 **alter services** exchange
positions N. 159–61 **thee,/'The Fortunate-Unhappy.'/Daylight**
F *thee, tht fortunate unhappy daylight* N. 161 **champian** variant of
'champaign,' 'open country.' 162 **politic authors** writers on government; F *pollticke* N. 163 **baffle** to subject (especially a knight)
to disgrace. 164 **point devise** perfectly correct. 165 **jade me** befool
me. 168 **in this** in this letter. 171 **strange** aloof. 172 **stout** brave,
proud.

with the swiftness of putting on. Jove and my stars
be praised. Here is yet a postscript.   174
[*Reads.*] 'Thou canst not choose but know who I
am. If thou entertain'st my love, let it appear in thy
smiling. Thy smiles become thee well. Therefore in my
presence still smile, dear my sweet, I prethee.'   178
Jove, I thank thee. I will smile, I will do everything
that thou wilt have me.   *Exit.*

Fabian. I will not give my part of this sport for a
pension of thousands to be paid from the Sophy.
Toby. I could marry this wench for this device.
Andrew. So could I too.   184
Toby. And ask no other dowry with her but such
another jest.

Enter Maria.

Andrew. Nor I neither.
Fabian. Here comes my noble gull-catcher.
Toby. Wilt thou set thy foot o' my neck?
Andrew. Or o' mine either?   190
Toby. Shall I play my freedom at tray-trip and be-
come thy bondslave?
Andrew. I' faith, or I either?
Toby. Why, thou hast put him in such a dream
that when the image of it leaves him, he must run
mad.   196
Maria. Nay, but say true, does it work upon him?
Toby. Like aqua-vite with a midwife.

173 Jove N. 178 still always. dear F *deero.* I prethee I pray thee.
182 the Sophy the shah of Persia N. 187 Nor I neither an emphatic
negative. 188 gull-catcher one who catches gulls; gulls are persons
easily tricked; compare 'gullible.' 189 Wilt . . . neck N. 191
play gamble. tray-trip a game of dice. 198 aqua-vite any distilled
liquor (Latin *aqua vitae*, 'water of life') N.

Maria. If you will then see the fruits of the sport, mark his first approach before my lady. He will come to her in yellow stockings, and 'tis a color she abhors; and cross-garter'd, a fashion she detests; and he will smile upon her, which will now be so unsuitable to her disposition, being addicted to a melancholy as she is, that it cannot but turn him into a notable contempt. If you will see it, follow me. 206

Toby. To the gates of Tartar, thou most excellent divel of wit.

Andrew. I'll make one too. *Exeunt.*

Finis, Actus secundus.

205–6 **a notable contempt** a state of being particularly despised (by Olivia). 207 **Tartar** Tartarus, the section of hell reserved for the most evil (Roman mythology). 208 **divel** devil. 209 **I'll make one too** I'll go along too.

Act III

SCENE 1

Enter Viola and Clown.

Viola. Save thee, friend, and thy music. Dost thou
live by thy tabor?

Clown. No, sir, I live by the church.

Viola. Art thou a churchman?   4

Clown. No such matter, sir. I do live by the church;
for I do live at my house, and my house doth stand
by the church.

Viola. So thou mayst say the king lies by a beggar,
if a beggar dwell near him; or the church stands by
thy tabor, if thy tabor stand by the church.   10

Clown. You have said, sir. To see this age! A sentence is but a chev'ril glove to a good wit. How
quickly the wrong side may be turn'd outward!

Viola. Nay, that's certain. They that dally nicely
with words may quickly make them wanton.   15

Clown. I would therefore my sister had had no
name, sir.

Viola. Why, man?

Clown. Why, sir, her name's a word, and to dally

---

1 Save thee God save thee. 2 live by make a living by. tabor
drum (which the stage clown commonly carried). 8 king F *kings.*
lies by dwells by. 11–12 A sentence any unit of meaning. a
chev'ril glove a kid glove. 14 dally nicely play foolishly or fastidi-
ously. 15 wanton capricious, unmanageable.

52

with that word might make my sister wanton. But
indeed words are very rascals since bonds disgrac'd
them.   22

Viola. Thy reason, man?

Clown. Troth, sir, I can yield you none without
words, and words are grown so false I am loath to
prove reason with them.   26

Viola. I warrant thou art a merry fellow and car'st
for nothing.

Clown. Not so, sir; I do care for something; but in
my conscience, sir, I do not care for you. If that be
to care for nothing, sir, I would it would make you
invisible.   32

Viola. Art not thou the Lady Olivia's fool?

Clown. No, indeed, sir. The Lady Olivia has no
folly. She will keep no fool, sir, till she be married;
and fools are as like husbands as pilchers are to her-
rings, the husbands the bigger. I am indeed not her
fool, but her corrupter of words.

Viola. I saw thee late at the Count Orsino's.   39

Clown. Foolery, sir, does walk about the orb like
the sun: it shines everywhere. I would be sorry, sir,
but the fool should be as oft with your master as with
my mistress. I think I saw your wisdom there.

Viola. Nay, and thou pass upon me, I'll no more
with thee. Hold, there's expenses for thee.   45
                                        [*Gives a coin.*]

20 **wanton** lascivious, lewd N. 21–2 **since bonds disgrac'd them** N.
24 **troth** truly. 25–6 **to prove reason** to test rightness. 27–8 **car'st
for nothing** you never worry. 36 **pilchers** pilchards, small fish related to the herring. 39 **late** lately. 40 **the orb** the world. 41
I would N. 43 **your wisdom** N. 44 **and thou pass upon me** if you
thrust at me (with your jokes). 45 **expenses** reimbursement.

Clown. Now Jove in his next commodity of hair
send thee a beard.

Viola. By my troth, I'll tell thee, I am almost sick
for one, though I would not have it grow on my chin.
Is thy lady within? 50

Clown. Would not a pair of these have bred, sir?

Viola. Yes, being kept together and put to use.

Clown. I would play Lord Pandarus of Phrygia, sir,
to bring a Cressida to this Troilus.

Viola. I understand you, sir. 'Tis well begg'd. 55
[*Gives another coin.*]

Clown. The matter, I hope, is not great, sir, beg-
ging but a beggar: Cressida was a beggar. My lady
is within, sir. I will conster to them whence you come.
Who you are and what you would are out of my
welkin. I might say 'element' but the word is over-
worn. *Exit.* 61

Viola. This fellow is wise enough to play the fool,
And to do that well craves a kind of wit.
He must observe their mood on whom he jests,
The quality of persons, and the time; 65
Not, like the haggard, check at every feather
That comes before his eye. This is a practice
As full of labor as a wise man's art;
For folly that he wisely shows is fit;

46 **Jove in his next commodity of hair** Jove when he next sends
a lot or assignment of hair. 51 **these** these coins. 52 **put to use**
loaned at interest. 53–4 **Pandarus . . . Cressida . . . Troilus** N.
57 **Cressida was a beggar** N. 58 **conster** construe, explain. 60
welkin sky. **element** both 'sky' and 'element' in the modern sense.
63 **craves a kind of wit** demands a kind of intelligence. 66 **Not,
like** F *And like.* the **haggard** the untrained hawk. **check at every
feather** forsake her quarry for other game. 67 **practice** skill. 69 **fit**
suitable.

But wise men, folly-fall'n, quite taint their wit.   70

Enter Sir Toby and [Sir] Andrew.

Toby. Save you, gentleman.

Viola. And you, sir.

Andrew. Dieu vous garde, monsieur.

Viola. Et vous aussi. Vostre serviteur.

Andrew. I hope, sir, you are, and I am yours.   75

Toby. Will you encounter the house? My niece is desirous you should enter, if your trade be to her.

Viola. I am bound to your niece, sir; I mean, she is the list of my voyage.   79

Toby. Taste your legs, sir; put them to motion.

Viola. My legs do better understand me, sir, than I understand what you mean by bidding me taste my legs.

Toby. I mean, to go, sir, to enter.   84

Viola. I will answer you with gait and entrance; but we are prevented.

Enter Olivia and Gentlewoman [Maria].

Most excellent accomplish'd lady, the heavens rain odors on you!

Andrew. [*Aside.*] That youth's a rare courtier. 'Rain odors.' Well!   90

70 **wise men** F *wisemens*. **folly-fall'n** when they have fallen into folly. 71 **Save you** God save you. 73–4 **Dieu . . . serviteur** God protect you, sir. . . . And you also. Your servant (French). 76 **encounter** meet, i.e. go into N. 77 **if your trade be to her** if your business concern her. 78 **bound to** bound for. 79 **list** limit, end. 80 **taste** try. 81–2 **understand** both 'comprehend' and 'stand under.' 85 **gait** walking; F *gate* N. 86 **prevented** anticipated. 87 **excellent** excellently.

Viola. My matter hath no voice, lady, but to your
own most pregnant and vouchsafed ear.

Andrew. [*Aside.*] 'Odors,' 'pregnant,' and 'vouchsafed.' I'll get 'em all three already.   94

Olivia. Let the garden door be shut and leave me
to my hearing. [*Exeunt Sir Toby, Sir Andrew, and
Maria.*] Give me your hand, sir.

Viola. My duty, madam, and most humble service.

Olivia. What is your name?   99

Viola. Cesario is your servant's name, fair princess.

Olivia. My servant, sir? 'Twas never merry world
Since lowly feigning was call'd compliment.
Y' are servant to the Count Orsino, youth.

Viola. And he is yours, and his must needs be yours.
Your servant's servant is your servant, madam.   105

Olivia. For him, I think not on him; for his thoughts,
Would they were blanks, rather than fill'd with me.

Viola. Madam, I come to whet your gentle thoughts
On his behalf.

Olivia.   O, by your leave, I pray you.
I bade you never speak again of him;   110
But would you undertake another suit,
I had rather hear you to solicit that
Than music from the spheres.

Viola.   Dear lady.

Olivia. Give me leave, beseech you. I did send,
After the last enchantment you did here,   115

91 hath no voice can be told no one. 92 pregnant receptive.
vouchsafed graciously given. 94 already fully prepared (for my
future use), all ready. 101–2 'Twas never . . . compliment N.
104 yours your servant (in love). his his servant. 107 blanks
blank thoughts. 108 to whet to sharpen (particularly by rubbing).
112 I had pronounced 'I'd.' 113 music from the spheres N. 114
beseech I beseech. 115 enchantment magic of making me love
you. here F *heare.*

A ring in chase of you. So did I abuse
Myself, my servant, and, I fear me, you.
Under your hard construction must I sit,
To force that on you in a shameful cunning
Which you knew none of yours. What might you
    think? 120
Have you not set mine honor at the stake
And baited it with all th' unmuzzled thoughts
That tyrannous heart can think? To one of your
    receiving
Enough is shown; a cypress, not a bosom,
Hides my heart. So let me hear you speak. 125
  Viola. I pity you.
  Olivia.   That's a degree to love.
  Viola. No, not a grize; for 'tis a vulgar proof
That very oft we pity enemies.
  Olivia. Why then methinks 'tis time to smile agen.
O world, how apt the poor are to be proud! 130
If one should be a prey, how much the better
To fall before the lion than the wolf!
                  Clock strikes.
The clock upbraids me with the waste of time.
Be not afraid, good youth; I will not have you. 134
And yet when wit and youth is come to harvest,
Your wife is like to reap a proper man.

116 abuse deceive. 118 construction interpretation (of my character). 119–20 To force . . . none of yours N. 121–2 at the stake . . . unmuzzled thoughts N. baited it harassed it. 123 your receiving your receptive capacity N. 124 a cypress a transparent black cloth used in sign of mourning. 125 Hides . . . speak N. 127 a grize a grece, a flight of steps, a degree. a vulgar proof a common experience. 129 'tis time to smile agen N. 132 the lion . . . the wolf N. 136 proper worthy, handsome.

There lies your way, due west.

Viola.   Then westward ho!
Grace and good disposition attend your ladyship.
You'll nothing, madam, to my lord by me?

Olivia. Stay.   140
I prethee tell me what thou think'st of me.

Viola. That you do think you are not what you are.

Olivia. If I think so, I think the same of you.

Viola. Then think you right. I am not what I am.

Olivia. I would you were as I would have you be.

Viola. Would it be better, madam, than I am?
I wish it might, for now I am your fool.

Olivia. O, what a deal of scorn looks beautiful
In the contempt and anger of his lip!   149
A murd'rous guilt shows not itself more soon
Than love that would seem hid: love's night is noon.
Cesario, by the roses of the spring,
By maidhood, honor, truth, and everything,
I love thee so, that maugre all thy pride,
Nor wit nor reason can my passion hide.   155
Do not extort thy reasons from this clause,
For that I woo, thou therefore hast no cause.
But rather reason thus with reason fetter:
Love sought is good, but given unsought is better.

Viola. By innocence I swear and by my youth,
I have one heart, one bosom, and one truth,   161
And that no woman has, nor never none

---

137 **due west. Then westward ho** N. 138 **disposition** frame of
mind. 142-3 **That you do think . . . the same of you** N. 147 **I am
your fool** you make a fool of me. 148 **what a deal** what a great
deal. 151 **love's night is noon** love makes itself plain. 154 **maugre**
despite. 155 **Nor . . . nor** neither . . . nor. 156-9 **Do not extort
. . . better** N. 162 **nor never none** nor ever one.

Shall mistress be of it, save I alone.
And so adieu, good madam. Never more
Will I my master's tears to you deplore.   165
   Olivia. Yet come again; for thou perhaps mayst
    move
That heart which now abhors, to like his love.

Exeunt.

SCENE 2

Enter Sir Toby, Sir Andrew, and Fabian.

   Andrew. No, faith, I'll not stay a jot longer.
   Toby. Thy reason, dear venom; give thy reason.
   Fabian. You must needs yield your reason, Sir
Andrew.   4
   Andrew. Marry, I saw your niece do more favors
to the Count's servingman than ever she bestow'd
upon me. I saw't i' th' orchard.
   Toby. Did she see the while, old boy? Tell me that.
   Andrew. As plain as I see you now.   9
   Fabian. This was a great argument of love in her
toward you.
   Andrew. 'Slight. Will you make an ass o' me?
   Fabian. I will prove it legitimate, sir, upon the
oaths of judgment and reason.   14
   Toby. And they have been grand-jurymen since
before Noah was a sailor.
   Fabian. She did show favor to the youth in your
sight only to exasperate you, to awake your dor-

167 his the Duke's. 2 **venom** venomous person N. 5 **Marry** to be
sure. 7 **orchard** probably 'garden' in the modern sense N. 8 **see**
watch N. 12 **'Slight** 'God's light,' an oath. 13 **legitimate** legiti-
mately, logically. 15 **grand-jurymen** competent to judge evidence.
18 **dormouse** i.e. sleepy N.

mouse valor, to put fire in your heart and brimstone
in your liver. You should then have accosted her;
and with some excellent jests, fire-new from the mint,
you should have bang'd the youth into dumbness.
This was look'd for at your hand, and this was
balk'd. The double gilt of this opportunity you let
time wash off, and you are now sail'd into the north
of my lady's opinion where you will hang like an
icicle on a Dutchman's beard, unless you do redeem
it by some laudable attempt either of valor or policy.

Andrew. And't be any way, it must be with valor,
for policy I hate. I had lief be a Brownist as a poli-
tician.   31

Toby. Why then, build me thy fortunes upon the
basis of valor. Challenge me the Count's youth to
fight with him; hurt him in eleven places. My niece
shall take note of it; and assure thyself there is no
love broker in the world can more prevail in man's
commendation with woman than report of valor.

Fabian. There is no way but this, Sir Andrew.

Andrew. Will either of you bear me a challenge to
him?   40

Toby. Go, write it in a martial hand. Be curst
and brief. It is no matter how witty, so it be elo-
quent and full of invention. Taunt him with the
license of ink. If thou thou'st him some thrice, it
shall not be amiss; and as many lies as will lie in
thy sheet of paper, although the sheet were big

19–20 **brimstone in your liver** make your liver hot. 21 **fire-new**
brand-new. 24 **balk'd** missed. **double gilt** N. 26–7 **an icicle on a
Dutchman's beard** N. 29 **And't** if it. 30 **Brownist** N. 32–3 **build
me . . . challenge me** ethical datives. 41 **curst** perversely cross.
43–4 **with the license of ink** with all the excessive liberty that
written language allows. 44 **If thou thou'st him** if you call him
'thou' N.

enough for the bed of Ware in England, set 'em
down, go about it. Let there be gall enough in thy
ink, though thou write with a goose-pen, no matter.
About it!   50

Andrew. Where shall I find you?

Toby. We'll call thee at the cubiculo. Go.

                                Exit Sir Andrew.

Fabian. This is a dear manikin to you, Sir Toby.

Toby. I have been dear to him, lad, some two thousand strong or so.   55

Fabian. We shall have a rare letter from him; but
you'll not deliver 't.

Toby. Never trust me then; and by all means stir
on the youth to an answer. I think oxen and wainropes cannot hale them together. For Andrew, if he
were open'd and you find so much blood in his liver
as will clog the foot of a flea, I'll eat the rest of th'
anatomy.

Fabian. And his opposite, the youth, bears in his
visage no great presage of cruelty.   65

Enter Maria.

Toby. Look where the youngest wren of mine comes.

Maria. If you desire the spleen and will laugh yourselves into stitches, follow me. Yond gull Malvolio
is turned heathen, a very renegatho; for there is no
Christian that means to be saved by believing rightly

---

47 the bed of Ware N. 48 gall N. 49 goose-pen N. 52 the cubiculo
the sleeping chamber (Latin *in cubiculo*). 53 dear manikin dear
little man N. 54 dear expensive. 59 wainropes wagon ropes.
60 hale haul. 61 blood in his liver i.e. courage N. 66 youngest
wren of mine N. 67 If you desire the spleen N. 68 gull dupe
69 renegatho renegade N.

can ever believe such impossible passages of grossness. He's in yellow stockings.   72

Toby. And cross-garter'd?

Maria. Most villainously, like a pedant that keeps
a school i' th' church. I have dogg'd him like his
murtherer. He does obey every point of the letter that
I dropp'd to betray him. He does smile his face into
more lines than is in the new map with the augmentation of the Indies. You have not seen such a thing as
'tis. I can hardly forbear hurling things at him. I
know my lady will strike him. If she do, he'll smile
and tak't for a great favor.   82

Toby. Come bring us, bring us where he is.

Exeunt omnes.

SCENE 3

Enter Sebastian and Antonio.

Sebastian. I would not by my will have troubled you,
But since you make your pleasure of your pains,
I will no further chide you.

Antonio. I could not stay behind you. My desire
(More sharp than filed steel) did spur me forth;
And not all love to see you (though so much   6
As might have drawn one to a longer voyage)
But jealousy what might befall your travel,
Being skilless in these parts; which to a stranger,
Unguided and unfriended, often prove   10
Rough and unhospitable. My willing love,

71–2 passages of grossness statements (in the letter) of exagger-
ated misinformation. 74 pedant schoolteacher. 76 murtherer
variant form of 'murderer.' 78–9 new map . . . Indies N. 6 all
love extreme desire. 8 jealousy solicitude. 9 skilless in without
knowledge of.

The rather by these arguments of fear,
Set forth in your pursuit.
   Sebastian.   My kind Antonio,
I can no other answer make but thanks,
And thanks; and ever oft good turns   15
Are shuffl'd off with such uncurrent pay.
But were my worth, as is my conscience, firm,
You should find better dealing. What's to do?
Shall we go see the relics of this town?
   Antonio. Tomorrow, sir. Best first go see your
     lodging?   20
   Sebastian. I am not weary and 'tis long to night.
I pray you let us satisfy our eyes
With the memorials and the things of fame
That do renown this city.
   Antonio.   Would you'ld pardon me.
I do not without danger walk these streets.   25
Once in a sea fight 'gainst the Count his galleys
I did some service of such note indeed
That, were I tane here, it would scarce be answer'd.
   Sebastian. Belike you slew great number of his
     people.   29
   Antonio. Th' offence is not of such a bloody nature,
Albeit the quality of the time and quarrel
Might well have given us bloody argument.
It might have since been answer'd in repaying
What we took from them, which for traffic's sake

15 And thanks . . . turns N. 16 shuffl'd off set aside, discounted.
uncurrent valueless as currency (i.e. 'thanks'). 17 my worth the
money I have. my conscience my conscience concerning your
favors. 19 relics monuments. 26 the Count his galleys the Count's
galleys. 28 tane taken. it would scarce be answer'd it would be
difficult to explain away. 29 Belike perhaps. 31 Albeit although.
34 for traffic's sake for trade's sake.

Most of our city did. Only myself stood out;　35
For which, if I be lapsed in this place,
I shall pay dear.

Sebastian.　　　Do not then walk too open.

Antonio. It doth not fit me. Hold, sir, here's my
　　purse.
In the south suburbs at the Elephant
Is best to lodge. I will bespeak our diet,　40
Whiles you beguile the time and feed your knowledge
With viewing of the town. There shall you have me.

Sebastian. Why I your purse?

Antonio. Haply your eye shall light upon some toy
You have desire to purchase; and your store　45
I think is not for idle markets, sir.

Sebastian. I'll be your purse-bearer and leave you
　　for
An hour.

Antonio. To th' Elephant.

Sebastian.　　　I do remember.

　　　　　　　　　　　　　Exeunt.

SCENE 4

Enter Olivia and Maria.

Olivia. I have sent after him; he says he'll come.
How shall I feast him? What bestow of him?
For youth is bought more oft than begg'd or bor-
　　row'd.

36 lapsed pounced upon as an offender. 39 the Elephant A London
inn sign N. 44 some toy some trifle. 45 store store of money.
46 idle markets useless purchasings. 2 of him on him (Cesario).

I speak too loud. Where's Malvolio? He is sad and
    civil, 4
And suits well for a servant with my fortunes.
Where is Malvolio?

Maria. He's coming, madam, but in very strange
manner. He is sure possess'd, madam.

Olivia. Why, what's the matter? Does he rave? 9

Maria. No, madam, he does nothing but smile. Your
ladyship were best to have some guard about you if
he come, for sure the man is tainted in's wits.

Olivia. Go call him hither.

Enter Malvolio.

               I am as mad as he,
If sad and merry madness equal be.
How now, Malvolio? 15

Malvolio. Sweet lady, ho, ho!

Olivia. Smil'st thou?
I sent for thee upon a sad occasion.

Malvolio. Sad lady, I could be sad. This does make
some obstruction in the blood, this cross-gartering;
but what of that? If it please the eye of one, it is
with me as the very true sonnet is, 'Please one and
please all.'

Olivia. Why, how doest thou, man? What is the
matter with thee? 25

Malvolio. Not black in my mind, though yellow in
my legs. It did come to his hands, and commands

4 **sad and civil** serious and sedate. 8 **possess'd** possessed by the
devil. 12 **in's** in his. 14 **sad** serious. 19 **sad** 'unhappy' and 'un-
comfortable.' 20 **this cross-gartering** N. 22 **sonnet** any short
poem. 22–3 **'Please one and please all'** N. 24 **Olivia. Why, how**
F *Mal. Why how.*

shall be executed. I think we do know the sweet
Roman hand.

Olivia. Wilt thou go to bed, Malvolio?   30

Malvolio. To bed? Ay, sweetheart, and I'll come
to thee.

Olivia. God comfort thee. Why dost thou smile so
and kiss thy hand so oft?

Maria. How do you, Malvolio?   35

Malvolio. At your request? Yes, nightingales answer
daws.

Maria. Why appear you with this ridiculous boldness before my lady?   39

Malvolio. 'Be not afraid of greatness.' 'Twas well
writ.

Olivia. What mean'st thou by that, Malvolio?

Malvolio. 'Some are born great.'

Olivia. Ha?

Malvolio. 'Some achieve greatness.'   45

Olivia. What say'st thou?

Malvolio. 'And some have greatness thrust upon
them.'

Olivia. Heaven restore thee.   49

Malvolio. 'Remember who commended thy yellow
stockings.'

Olivia. Thy yellow stockings?

Malvolio. 'And wish'd to see thee cross-garter'd.'

Olivia. Cross-garter'd?   54

Malvolio. 'Go to, thou art made, if thou desir'st
to be so.'

Olivia. Am I made?

Malvolio. 'If not, let me see thee a servant still.'

29 **Roman hand** the Italian style, like modern handwriting N.
36–7 **At your request . . . daws** N. 55 **Go to** go on. **made** N.

Olivia. Why, this is very midsummer madness.

Enter Servant.

Servant. Madam, the young gentleman of the Count Orsino's is return'd. I could hardly entreat him back. He attends your ladyship's pleasure.   62

Olivia. I'll come to him. [*Exit Servant.*] Good Maria, let this fellow be look'd to. Where's my cousin Toby? Let some of my people have a special care of him. I would not have him miscarry for the half of my dowry.   *Exit [Olivia with Maria].*   67

Malvolio. O, ho, do you come near me now? No worse man than Sir Toby to look to me. This concurs directly with the letter. She sends him on purpose that I may appear stubborn to him, for she incites me to that in the letter. 'Cast thy humble slough,' says she. 'Be opposite with a kinsman, surly with servants. Let thy tongue tang with arguments of state. Put thyself into the trick of singularity.' And consequently sets down the manner how: as, a sad face, a reverend carriage, a slow tongue, in the habit of some sir of note, and so forth. I have lim'd her, but it is Jove's doing and Jove make me thankful. And when she went away now, 'Let this fellow be look'd to.' Fellow? Not 'Malvolio,' nor after my degree, but 'fellow.' Why, everything adheres to-

---

59 **midsummer madness** N. 66 **miscarry** come to harm. 71 **stubborn** hard, stiff, rigid. 74 **tang with** sound with, echo with; F *langer with* N. 76–8 **And consequently . . . and so forth** N. 77 **sad** serious. 77–8 **the habit of some sir** the clothing of some gentleman. 78 **lim'd** caught N. 81 **fellow** probably in the sense of 'companion,' not as Olivia uses it in addressing an inferior. 82 **degree** position. **togither** together.

gither, that no dram of a scruple, no scruple of a
scruple, no obstacle, no incredulous or unsafe circumstance—what can be said? Nothing that can
be, can come between me and the full prospect of my
hopes. Well, Jove, not I, is the doer of this and he
is to be thanked.   88

Enter [Sir] Toby, Fabian, and Maria.

Toby. Which way is he, in the name of sanctity?
If all the divels of hell be drawn in little and Legion
himself possess'd him, yet I'll speak to him.   91

Fabian. Here he is, here he is. How is't with you,
sir? How is't with you, man?

Malvolio. Go off, I discard you. Let me enjoy my
private. Go off.   95

Maria. Lo, how hollow the fiend speaks within him.
Did I not tell you? Sir Toby, my lady prays you to
have a care of him.

Malvolio. Ah, ha, does she so?   99

Toby. Go to, go to; peace, peace; we must deal
gently with him. Let me alone. How do you, Malvolio? How is't with you? What, man, defy the divel?
Consider, he's an enemy to mankind.

Malvolio. Do you know what you say?   104

Maria. La you, and you speak ill of the divel, how
he takes it at heart. Pray God he be not bewitch'd.

Fabian. Carry his water to th' wise woman.

Maria. Marry, and it shall be done tomorrow morn-

---

83 dram one-eighth fluid ounce. scruple both 'doubt' and 'one
twenty-fourth of an ounce' (apothecaries' weight). 84 incredulous
incredible. 90 drawn in little brought together in a small space N.
Legion N. 93 How is't with you, man? N. 95 private privacy.
100 Go to go on. 105 La Oh! and if. 106 bewitch'd N. 107 Carry
. . . woman N.

ing if I live. My lady would not lose him for more
than I'll say.   110

Malvolio. How now, mistress?

Maria. O Lord.

Toby. Prethee, hold thy peace. This is not the way.
Do you not see you move him? Let me alone with him.

Fabian. No way but gentleness; gently, gently. The
fiend is rough and will not be roughly us'd.   116

Toby. Why, how now my bawcock? How dost thou,
chuck?

Malvolio. Sir.   119

Toby. Ay, biddy, come with me. What, man, 'tis not
for gravity to play at cherry-pit with Satan. Hang
him, foul collier!

Maria. Get him to say his prayers; good Sir Toby,
get him to pray.

Malvolio. My prayers, minx?   125

Maria. No, I warrant you, he will not hear of god-
liness.

Malvolio. Go hang yourselves all. You are idle
shallow things. I am not of your element. You shall
know more hereafter.   *Exit.*

Toby. Is't possible?   131

Fabian. If this were play'd upon a stage now, I
could condemn it as an improbable fiction.

Toby. His very genius hath taken the infection of
the device, man.   135

Maria. Nay, pursue him now, lest the device take
air and taint.

---

113 **Prethee** I pray thee. 117 **bawcock** good fellow (French *beau
coq*). 118 **chuck** chick. 120 **biddy** chicken. 121 **gravity** dignity.
cherry-pit a child's game N. 122 **collier** coal peddler N. 128 **idle**
empty, trifling. 134 **genius** nature. 136–7 **take air and taint** be
exposed and thus contaminated.

Fabian. Why, we shall make him mad indeed.

Maria. The house will be the quieter.   139

Toby. Come, we'll have him in a dark room and bound. My niece is already in the belief that he's mad. We may carry it thus for our pleasure and his penance, till our very pastime, tired out of breath, prompt us to have mercy on him; at which time we will bring the device to the bar and crown thee for a finder of madmen. But see, but see.   146

Enter Sir Andrew.

Fabian. More matter for a May morning.

Andrew. Here's the challenge; read it. I warrant there's vinegar and pepper in't.

Fabian. Is't so saucy?   150

Andrew. Ay, is't? I warrant him. Do but read.

Toby. Give me. [*Reads.*] 'Youth, whatsoever thou art, thou art but a scurvy fellow.'

Fabian. Good and valiant.   154

Toby. [*Reads.*] 'Wonder not nor admire not in thy mind why I do call thee so, for I will show thee no reason for't.'

Fabian. A good note that keeps you from the blow of the law.   159

Toby. [*Reads.*] 'Thou com'st to the Lady Olivia, and in my sight she uses thee kindly. But thou liest in thy throat; that is not the matter I challenge thee for.'

Fabian. Very brief and to exceeding good sense—less.   165

140–1 in a dark room and bound N. 142 carry it carry the trick on. 145 the bar the bar of judgment. 147 matter for a May morning material for a May-day comedy. 150 saucy a quibble on 'spicy' and 'impudent' or 'sharp.' 151 Ay, is't? F *I, ist?* 153 scurvy scabby, dirty. 158–9 A good note . . . law N.

Toby. [*Reads.*] 'I will waylay thee going home;
where if it be thy chance to kill me—'

Fabian. Good.

Toby. [*Reads.*] 'Thou kill'st me like a rogue and
a villain.'   170

Fabian. Still you keep o' th' windy side of the law.
Good.

Toby. [*Reads.*] 'Fare thee well, and God have mercy
upon one of our souls. He may have mercy upon
mine, but my hope is better, and so look to thyself.
Thy friend as thou usest him, and thy sworn enemy,
                                        'Andrew Aguecheek.'

If this letter move him not, his legs cannot. I'll give't
him.   179

Maria. You may have very fit occasion for't. He
is now in some commerce with my lady and will by
and by depart.   182

Toby. Go, Sir Andrew. Scout me for him at the
corner of the orchard like a bumbaily. So soon as
ever thou seest him, draw; and as thou draw'st,
swear horrible; for it comes to pass oft that a terrible oath with a swaggering accent sharply twang'd
off, gives manhood more approbation then ever proof
itself would have earn'd him. Away.   189

Andrew. Nay, let me alone for swearing.   *Exit.*

Toby. Now will not I deliver his letter; for the
behavior of the young gentleman gives him out to
be of good capacity and breeding; his employment
between his lord and my niece confirms no less. There-

171 windy windward, safe. 175 my hope my hope of winning.
180 You may F *Yon may.* for't F *fot't.* 181–2 by and by immediately, soon. 183 me ethical dative. 184 **orchard** probably 'garden.'
bumbaily bumbailiff, an agent employed in making arrests. 188
approbation confirmation. **proof** testing. 190 **let me alone leave
that** (swearing) to me.

fore this letter, being so excellently ignorant, will
breed no terror in the youth. He will find it comes
from a clodpoll. But, sir, I will deliver his challenge
by word of mouth, set upon Aguecheek a notable
report of valor, and drive the gentleman (as I know
his youth will aptly receive it) into a most hideous
opinion of his rage, skill, fury, and impetuosity.
This will so fright them both that they will kill one
another by the look, like cockatrices.   203

Enter Olivia and Viola.

Fabian. Here he comes with your niece. Give them
way till he take leave, and presently after him.

Toby. I will meditate the while upon some horrid
message for a challenge.

[*Exeunt Sir Toby, Fabian, and Maria.*]

Olivia. I have said too much unto a heart of stone,
And laid mine honor too unchary on't.   209
There's something in me that reproves my fault;
But such a headstrong potent fault it is
That it but mocks reproof.

Viola. With the same havior that your passion
            bears,
Goes on my master's griefs.

Olivia. Here, wear this jewel for me; 'tis my pic-
            ture.   215
Refuse it not; it hath no tongue to vex you.
And I beseech you come again tomorrow.

197 **a clodpoll** a clod-head, a fool. 203 **cockatrices** basilisks N.
204–5 **Give them way** give them privacy, let them alone. 205
presently immediately. 209 **unchary on't** carelessly on it (the
heart of stone). 213 **havior** behavior. 214 **Goes . . . griefs** my
master's grieving love for you goes on N. 215 **jewel** any ornament
or trinket; here perhaps 'locket.'

What shall you ask of me that I'll deny,
That honor, sav'd, may upon asking give?
　Viola. Nothing but this: your true love for my mas-
　　ter. 220
　Olivia. How with mine honor may I give him that
Which I have given to you?
　Viola.　　　　　　 I will acquit you.
　Olivia. Well, come again tomorrow. Fare thee well.
A fiend like thee might bear my soul to hell. [*Exit.*]

Enter [Sir] Toby and Fabian.

　Toby. Gentleman, God save thee. 225
　Viola. And you, sir.
　Toby. That defense thou hast, betake thee to't. Of
what nature the wrongs are thou hast done him, I
know not; but thy intercepter, full of despite, bloody
as the hunter, attends thee at the orchard end. Dismount thy tuck, be yare in thy preparation; for thy
assailant is quick, skillful, and deadly. 232
　Viola. You mistake, sir. I am sure no man hath any
quarrel to me. My remembrance is very free and
clear from any image of offense done to any man.
　Toby. You'll find it otherwise, I assure you. Therefore, if you hold your life at any price, betake you
to your guard; for your opposite hath in him what
youth, strength, skill, and wrath can furnish man
withal. 240
　Viola. I pray you, sir, what is he?
　Toby. He is knight dubb'd with unhatch'd rapier

---

219 honor, sav'd honor preserved. 227 betake thee to't F *betake
the too't.* 229 despite scorn, defiance. 230–1 Dismount thy tuck
take out thy rapier. 231 yare quick. 240 withal with. 242–3 with
unhatch'd rapier . . . carpet consideration N.

and on carpet consideration, but he is a divel in private brawl. Souls and bodies hath he divorc'd three; and his incensement at this moment is so implacable that satisfaction can be none but by pangs of death and sepulcher. 'Hob, nob' is his word. 'Give't or take't.'   248

Viola. I will return again into the house and desire some conduct of the lady. I am no fighter. I have heard of some kind of men that put quarrels purposely on others to taste their valor. Belike this is a man of that quirk.   253

Toby. Sir, no. His indignation derives itself out of a very competent injury; therefore get you on and give him his desire. Back you shall not to the house, unless you undertake that with me which with as much safety you might answer him. Therefore on, or strip your sword stark naked; for meddle you must, that's certain, or forswear to wear iron about you.

Viola. This is as uncivil as strange. I beseech you, do me this courteous office, as to know of the knight what my offense to him is. It is something of my negligence, nothing of my purpose.   264

Toby. I will do so. Signior Fabian, stay you by this gentleman till my return.   *Exit Toby.*

Viola. Pray you, sir, do you know of this matter?

Fabian. I know the knight is incens'd against you,

---

247 **Hob, nob** have or have not, give or take. 250 **conduct** protective escort. 252 **Belike** probably, possibly. 253 quirk peculiarity. 255 **competent injury** sufficiently serious injury; F *computent*. 257–8 **unless you undertake . . . answer him** N. 259 **meddle** engage (in the fight). 260 **forswear to wear iron** repudiate on oath (your right) to wear a sword. 262 **to know of the knight** to find out from the knight.

even to a mortal arbitrement; but nothing of the
circumstance more.   270

Viola. I beseech you, what manner of man is he?

Fabian. Nothing of that wonderful promise, to read
him by his form, as you are like to find him in the
proof of his valor. He is indeed, sir, the most skillful,
bloody, and fatal opposite that you could possibly
have found in any part of Illyria. Will you walk
towards him? I will make your peace with him if I
can.   278

Viola. I shall be much bound to you for't. I am one
that had rather go with sir priest than sir knight. I
care not who knows so much of my mettle.   *Exeunt.*

Enter [Sir] Toby and [Sir] Andrew.

Toby. Why, man, he's a very divel; I have not seen
such a firago. I had a pass with him, rapier, scab-
bard, and all, and he gives me the stuck-in with such
a mortal motion that it is inevitable; and on the
answer he pays you as surely as your feet hits the
ground they step on. They say he has been fencer
to the Sophy.

Andrew. Pox on't, I'll not meddle with him.   289

Toby. Ay, but he will not now be pacified. Fabian
can scarce hold him yonder.

Andrew. Plague on't, and I thought he had been
valiant and so cunning in fence, I'd have seen him

269 **mortal arbitrement** deadly settlement. 274 **proof** testing. 280 **sir priest** i.e. 'dominus,' a common title of address for the clergy. 281 **mettle** quality of temperament. 283 **firago** virago N. **pass** bout. 284 **the stuck-in** the thrust or lunge. 285–6 **the answer** the return hit. 286 **hits** N. 288 **the Sophy** the shah of Persia. 289 **Pox on't** the plague on it N. 292 and if.

damn'd ere I'd have challeng'd him. Let him let the
matter slip, and I'll give him my horse, grey Capilet.

Toby. I'll make the motion. Stand here; make a
good show on't. This shall end without the perdition
of souls. [*Aside.*] Marry, I'll ride your horse as well
as I ride you.   299

Enter Fabian and Viola.

I have his horse to take up the quarrel. I have persuaded him the youth's a divel.   301

Fabian. He is as horribly conceited of him, and
pants and looks pale as if a bear were at his heels.

Toby. There's no remedy, sir. He will fight with you
for's oath sake. Marry, he hath better bethought him
of his quarrel, and he finds that now scarce to be
worth talking of. Therefore draw for the supportance of his vow. He protests he will not hurt you.

Viola. [*Aside.*] Pray God defend me! A little thing
would make me tell them how much I lack of a man.

Fabian. Give ground if you see him furious.   311

Toby. Come, Sir Andrew, there's no remedy. The
gentleman will for his honor's sake have one bout
with you. He cannot by the duello avoid it; but he
has promised me as he is a gentleman and a soldier,
he will not hurt you. Come on, to't.   316

Andrew. Pray God he keep his oath!   [*Draws.*]

Enter Antonio.

Viola. I do assure you 'tis against my will. [*Draws.*]

295 Capilet N. 297–8 the perdition of souls i.e. killing. 300 to
take up to settle. 302 He is as horribly conceited of him he is
imagining all sorts of dreadful things about him. 305 for's for his.
307 supportance keeping. 314 the duello the rules of polite dueling N.

Antonio. Put up your sword. If this young gentle-
    man
Have done offense, I take the fault on me;   320
If you offend him, I for him defy you.

Toby. You, sir? Why, what are you?

Antonio. [*Draws.*] One, sir, that for his love dares
    yet do more
Than you have heard him brag to you he will.   324

Toby. Nay, if you be an undertaker, I am for you.
                        [*Draws.*]

Enter Officers.

Fabian. O good Sir Toby, hold. Here come the
officers.

Toby. [*To Antonio.*] I'll be with you anon.

Viola. [*To Sir Andrew.*] Pray, sir, put your sword
up, if you please.   330

Andrew. Marry, will I, sir; and for that I promis'd
you, I'll be as good as my word. He will bear you
easily and reins well.

1 Officer. This is the man; do thy office.

2 Officer. Antonio, I arrest thee at the suit   335
Of Count Orsino.

Antonio.   You do mistake me, sir.

1 Officer. No, sir, no jot. I know your favor well,
Though now you have no sea cap on your head.
Take him away. He knows I know him well.

Antonio. I must obey. [*To Viola.*] This comes with
    seeking you.   340
But there's no remedy; I shall answer it.
What will you do, now my necessity

---

325 **an undertaker** one who takes up a challenge. 328 **anon** presently. 331 **and for that** and for the horse. 333 **reins** F *raines.*
337 **favor** face.

Makes me to ask you for my purse? It grieves me
Much more for what I cannot do for you
Than what befalls myself. You stand amaz'd,   345
But be of comfort.

  2 Officer. Come, sir, away.

  Antonio. I must entreat of you some of that money.

  Viola. What money, sir?
For the fair kindness you have show'd me here,   350
And part being prompted by your present trouble,
Out of my lean and low ability
I'll lend you something. My having is not much;
I'll make division of my present with you.   354
Hold, there's half my coffer.

  Antonio.   Will you deny me now?
Is't possible that my deserts to you
Can lack persuasion? Do not tempt my misery,
Lest that it make me so unsound a man
As to upbraid you with those kindnesses
That I have done for you.

  Viola.   I know of none,   360
Nor know I you by voice or any feature.
I hate ingratitude more in a man
Than lying, vainness, babbling drunkenness,
Or any taint of vice whose strong corruption
Inhabits our frail blood.

  Antonio.   O heavens themselves!   365

  2 Officer. Come, sir, I pray you go.

  Antonio. Let me speak a little. This youth that you
    see here

345 amaz'd 'dazed,' stronger than in modern usage. 351 **part** in
part. 353 **My having** what I have. 354 **my present** what I have
now. 355 **my coffer** my money. 356 **my deserts to you** what you
owe me. 357 **persuasion** the power to persuade. 363 **vainness**
'uselessness' or 'personal conceit.'

I snatch'd one half out of the jaws of death;
Reliev'd him with such sanctity of love;
And to his image which methought did promise 370
Most venerable worth, did I devotion.

1 Officer. What's that to us? The time goes by.
　Away.

Antonio. But O, how vild an idol proves this god!
Thou hast, Sebastian, done good feature shame.
In nature there's no blemish but the mind. 375
None can be called deform'd but the unkind.
.Virtue is beauty; but the beauteous evil
Are empty trunks, o'erflourish'd by the devil.

1 Officer. The man grows mad; away with him.
　Come, come, sir. 379

Antonio. Lead me on.　　*Exit [with Officers].*

Viola. Methinks his words do from such passion fly
That he believes himself; so do not I.
Prove true, imagination, O, prove true,
That I, dear brother, be now tane for you! 384

Toby. Come hither, knight; come hither, Fabian.
We'll whisper o'er a couplet or two of most sage saws.

Viola. He nam'd Sebastian. I my brother know
Yet living in my glass. Even such and so
In favor was my brother, and he went
Still in this fashion, color, ornament, 390

---

370 **image** appearance N. 371 **venerable** worthy of veneration.
373 **vild** vile N. 376 **unkind** 'cruel' and 'unnatural.' 377 **beauteous evil** evil beautiful in appearance. 378 **empty trunks, o'erflourish'd** empty bodies covered with blossoms or verdure N. 381 **fly** come violently. 382 **so do not I** 'I do not believe him,' and 'I do not believe myself' (in the hope that my brother is alive). 384 **tane** taken. 386 **sage saws** wise sayings. 388 **Yet living in my glass** i.e. whenever I look in the mirror. 389 **favor** face. 390 **still** always.

For him I imitate. O, if it prove,
Tempests are kind, and salt waves fresh in love!
[*Exit.*]

Toby. A very dishonest paltry boy, and more a
coward than a hare. His dishonesty appears in leaving his friend here in necessity and denying him; and
for his cowardship, ask Fabian.   396

Fabian. A coward, a most devout coward; religious
in it.

Andrew. 'Slid, I'll after him again and beat him.

Toby. Do; cuff him soundly, but never draw thy
sword.   401

Andrew. And I do not.

Fabian. Come, let's see the event.

Toby. I dare lay any money 'twill be nothing yet.
Exeunt.

[*Finis, Actus tertius.*]

391 **For** because. **it** that he is alive. 393 **dishonest** dishonorable.
394 **hare** N. 399 **'Slid** 'God's lid' (eyelid); a mild oath. 402 **And** if.
403 **the event** the result, the outcome. 404 **yet** nevertheless.
Exeunt F *Exit.*

Act IV

SCENE 1

Enter Sebastian and Clown.

Clown. Will you make me believe that I am not sent for you?

Sebastian. Go to, go to, thou art a foolish fellow. Let me be clear of thee. 4

Clown. Well held out, i' faith. No, I do not know you; nor I am not sent to you by my lady to bid you come speak with her; nor your name is not Master Cesario; nor this is not my nose neither. Nothing that is so is so. 9

Sebastian. I prethee vent thy folly somewhere else. Thou know'st not me.

Clown. Vent my folly! He has heard that word of some great man and now applies it to a fool. Vent my folly! I am afraid this great lubber the world will prove a cockney. I prethee now ungird thy strangeness, and tell me what I shall vent to my lady? Shall I vent to her that thou art coming? 17

Sebastian. I prethee, foolish Greek, depart from me. There's money for thee. If you tarry longer,

---

3 Go to go on. 5 held out kept up, continued. 10 I prethee I pray thee. 14 lubber lout. 15 a cockney an affected, foppish person N. ungird thy strangeness let loose thy strange manner. 18 Greek 'merry companion' or 'unintelligible speaker.'

I shall give worse payment. 20

Clown. By my troth, thou hast an open hand. These wise men that give fools money get themselves a good report, after fourteen years' purchase. 23

Enter [Sir] Andrew, [Sir] Toby, and Fabian.

Andrew. Now, sir, have I met you again. There's for you. [*Strikes Sebastian.*]

Sebastian. Why, there's for thee, and there, and there. 26

Are all the people mad? [*Beats Sir Andrew.*]

Toby. Hold, sir, or I'll throw your dagger o'er the house. [*Holds Sebastian.*]

Clown. This will I tell my lady straight. I would not be in some of your coats for twopence. [*Exit.*]

Toby. Come on, sir; hold. 32

Andrew. Nay, let him alone. I'll go another way to work with him. I'll have an action of battery against him if there be any law in Illyria. Though I stroke him first, yet it's no matter for that. 36

Sebastian. Let go thy hand.

Toby. Come, sir, I will not let you go. Come, my young soldier, put up your iron. You are well flesh'd. Come on. 40

Sebastian. I will be free from thee. [*Frees himself.*]
What wouldst thou now?

If thou dar'st tempt me further, draw thy sword.
[*Draws.*]

Toby. What, what? Nay then, I must have an ounce

23 after fourteen years' purchase at a high price N. 34 action of battery a suit at law for beating (me). 35 stroke struck. 39 You are well flesh'd you have had a good taste N.

82

or two of this malapert blood from you.   [*Draws.*]

Enter Olivia.

Olivia. Hold, Toby. On thy life I charge thee, hold.
Toby. Madam.   46
Olivia. Will it be ever thus? Ungracious wretch,
Fit for the mountains and the barbarous caves,
Where manners ne'er were preach'd. Out of my sight.
Be not offended, dear Cesario.   50
Rudesby, be gone.

     [*Exeunt Sir Toby, Sir Andrew, and Fabian.*]
                    I prethee, gentle friend,
Let thy fair wisdom, not thy passion, sway
In this uncivil and unjust extent
Against thy peace. Go with me to my house,
And hear thou there how many fruitless pranks   55
This ruffian hath botch'd up, that thou thereby
Mayst smile at this. Thou shalt not choose but go.
Do not deny. Beshrew his soul for me.
He started one poor heart of mine, in thee.
Sebastian. What relish is in this? How runs the
     stream?   60
Or am I mad, or else this is a dream.
Let fancy still my sense in Lethe steep;
If it be thus to dream, still let me sleep.
Olivia. Nay, come, I prethee. Would thou'dst be
     rul'd by me?
Sebastian. Madam, I will.

44 **malapert** impudent. 51 **Rudesby** unmannerly fellow. 52 **fair**
just. **sway** rule. 53 **uncivil** uncivilized. **extent** probably 'display,'
possibly 'assault.' 58 **beshrew** curse. 59 **started** startled. **heart**
'heart' and 'hart' N. 60 **relish** taste. 61 **Or . . . or** either . . . or.
62 **Lethe** the river of forgetfulness in the underworld (Greek
mythology). 63 **still** always.

Olivia.   O, say so, and so be.   65
                             Exeunt.

SCENE 2

Enter Maria and Clown.

Maria. Nay, I prethee put on this gown and this
beard. Make him believe thou art Sir Topas the curate. Do it quickly. I'll call Sir Toby the whilst.
                                              [*Exit.*]
Clown. Well, I'll put it on, and I will dissemble myself in't, and I would I were the first that ever dis-
sembled in such a gown. I am not tall enough to
become the function well, nor lean enough to be
thought a good student; but to be said an honest
man and a good housekeeper goes as fairly as to say
a careful man and a great scholar. The competitors
enter.   11

Enter [Sir] Toby [and Maria].

Toby. Jove bless thee, Master Parson.
Clown. Bonos dies, Sir Toby; for as the old hermit
of Prague that never saw pen and ink very wittily
said to a niece of King Gorboduc, 'That that is is';
so I being Master Parson, am Master Parson. For
what is 'that' but that? And 'is' but is?   17
Toby. To him, Sir Topas.

2 Sir common title of address for the clergy. Topas N. 3 the
whilst meanwhile. 4 dissemble disguise. 7 the function the function of a cleric. 8 student student. 9 a good housekeeper one
who lives well. 10 the competitors the associates. 13 Bonos dies
good day (a pretense at ecclesiastical Latin). 13–14 the old hermit
of Prague probably the clown's invention. 15 King Gorboduc N.

Clown. What ho, I say. Peace in this prison. 19
Toby. The knave counterfeits well; a good knave.
Malvolio within.

Malvolio. Who calls there?

Clown. Sir Topas the curate, who comes to visit Malvolio the lunatic.

Malvolio. Sir Topas, Sir Topas, good Sir Topas, go to my lady. 25

Clown. Out, hyperbolical fiend! How vexest thou this man? Talkest thou nothing but of ladies?

Toby. Well said, Master Parson.

Malvolio. Sir Topas, never was man thus wronged; good Sir Topas, do not think I am mad. They have laid me here in hideous darkness. 31

Clown. Fie, thou dishonest Satan. I call thee by the most modest terms, for I am one of those gentle ones that will use the divel himself with courtesy. Say'st thou that house is dark? 35

Malvolio. As hell, Sir Topas.

Clown. Why, it hath bay windows transparent as barricadoes, and the clear stores toward the south north are as lustrous as ebony. And yet complainest thou of obstruction? 40

Malvolio. I am not mad, Sir Topas; I say to you this house is dark.

Clown. Madman, thou errest. I say there is no darkness but ignorance, in which thou art more puzzl'd than the Egyptians in their fog. 45

---

20 **knave** boy, fellow. 20 SD **Malvolio within** N. 26 **hyperbolical** enormous. 32 **dishonest** dishonorable. 33 **modest** moderate. 35 **house** 'house' and 'darkened room.' 38 **barricadoes** barricades. **clear stores** clerestories, the upper part of a church or building with a series of windows. 45 **the Egyptians in their fog** N.

Malvolio. I say this house is as dark as ignorance, though ignorance were as dark as hell; and I say there was never man thus abus'd. I am no more mad than you are; make the trial of it in any constant question. 50

Clown. What is the opinion of Pythagoras concerning wild fowl?

Malvolio. That the soul of our grandam might happily inhabit a bird.

Clown. What think'st thou of his opinion? 55

Malvolio. I think nobly of the soul and no way approve his opinion.

Clown. Fare thee well. Remain thou still in darkness. Thou shalt hold th' opinion of Pythagoras ere I will allow of thy wits, and fear to kill a woodcock, lest thou dispossess the soul of thy grandam. Fare thee well.

Malvolio. Sir Topas, Sir Topas.

Toby. My most exquisite Sir Topas.

Clown. Nay, I am for all waters. 65

Maria. Thou mightst have done this without thy beard and gown. He sees thee not.

Toby. To him in thine own voice, and bring me word how thou find'st him. [*To Maria.*] I would we were well rid of this knavery. If he may be conveniently deliver'd, I would he were; for I am now so far in offense with my niece that I cannot pursue with any safety this sport to the upshot. [*To the Clown.*] Come by and by to my chamber. *Exit* [*with Maria*].

49 constant consistent. 51 Pythagoras N. 53 happily haply, by chance. 65 for all waters good for any trade, occupation. 71 deliver'd let out. 73 this sport to the upshot this sport to the outcome N. to F omits. 74 by and by immediately.

Clown. [*Sings.*]

> Hey Robin, jolly Robin,   75
> Tell me how thy lady does.

Malvolio. Fool.

Clown. 'My lady is unkind, perdie.'

Malvolio. Fool.

Clown. 'Alas, why is she so?'   80

Malvolio. Fool, I say.

Clown. 'She loves another.' Who calls, ha?

Malvolio. Good fool, as ever thou wilt deserve well
at my hand, help me to a candle, and pen, ink, and
paper. As I am a gentleman, I will live to be thankful
to thee for't.   86

Clown. Master Malvolio?

Malvolio. Ay, good fool.

Clown. Alas, sir, how fell you besides your five wits?

Malvolio. Fool, there was never man so notoriously
abus'd. I am as well in my wits, fool, as thou art.   91

Clown. But as well: then you are mad indeed, if
you be no better in your wits than a fool.

Malvolio. They have here propertied me; keep me
in darkness, send ministers to me, asses, and do all
they can to face me out of my wits.   96

Clown. Advise you what you say. The minister is
here. Malvolio, Malvolio, thy wits the heavens restore. Endeavor thyself to sleep, and leave thy vain
bibble babble.   100

Malvolio. Sir Topas.

Clown. Maintain no words with him, good fellow.

75 Hey Robin N. 78 perdie certainly (French *par dieu*). 89 how
fell you besides how fell you out of. five wits N. 94 propertied me
made me a property, a mere thing. 96 face me out of my wits
impudently claim that I am mad. 97 Advise you be careful of.

Who, I, sir? Not I, sir. God buy you, good Sir Topas.
Marry, amen. I will, sir, I will.

Malvolio. Fool, fool, fool, I say.   105

Clown. Alas, sir, be patient. What say you, sir? I
am shent for speaking to you.

Malvolio. Good fool, help me to some light and
some paper. I tell thee I am as well in my wits as
any man in Illyria.   110

Clown. Well-a-day, that you were, sir.

Malvolio. By this hand, I am. Good fool, some ink,
paper, and light; and convey what I will set down to
my lady. It shall advantage thee more than ever the
bearing of letter did.   115

Clown. I will help you to't. But tell me true, are you
not mad indeed? Or do you but counterfeit?

Malvolio. Believe me, I am not; I tell thee true.

Clown. Nay, I'll ne'er believe a madman till I see
his brains. I will fetch you light and paper and ink.

Malvolio. Fool, I'll requite it in the highest   121
degree. I prethee be gone.

Clown. [*Sings.*]

> I am gone, sir,
> And anon, sir,
> I'll be with you again.   125
>   In a trice,
>   Like to the old Vice,
> Your need to sustain.
> Who with dagger of lath,
> In his rage and his wrath,   130
>   Cries 'Ah, ha,' to the divel.

103 God buy you good-by N. 104 Marry N. 107 shent reproved.
111 Well-a-day woe, alas. 114 advantage be of advantage to.
124 anon straightway, at once. 123–5 I am gone, sir . . . again
N. 127–33 Like to the old Vice . . . 'Pare thy nails, dad' N.

Like a mad lad,
'Pare thy nails, dad.'
Adieu, goodman divel.

Exit.

SCENE 3

Enter Sebastian.

Sebastian. This is the air; that is the glorious sun;
This pearl she gave me, I do feel't and see't;
And though 'tis wonder that enwraps me thus,
Yet 'tis not madness. Where's Antonio then?
I could not find him at the Elephant;   5
Yet there he was, and there I found this credit
That he did range the town to seek me out.
His counsel now might do me golden service;
For though my soul disputes well with my sense
That this may be some error, but no madness,   10
Yet doth this accident and flood of fortune
So far exceed all instance, all discourse,
That I am ready to distrust mine eyes
And wrangle with my reason that persuades me
To any other trust but that I am mad,   15
Or else the lady's mad. Yet if 'twere so,
She could not sway her house, command her fol-
      lowers,
Take and give back affairs and their dispatch

134 Adieu, goodman divel N. 6 this credit this report believed.
9 my soul disputes well with my sense my mind agrees well with
my senses. 12 instance example. discourse logic, reason. 14
wrangle dispute. 17 sway rule. 18 dispatch management.

With such a smooth, discreet, and stable bearing
As I perceive she does. There's something in't   20
That is deceivable. But here the lady comes.

Enter Olivia and Priest.

Olivia. Blame not this haste of mine. If you mean
    well,
Now go with me and with this holy man
Into the chantry by. There before him
And underneath that consecrated roof,   25
Plight me the full assurance of your faith,
That my most jealous and too doubtful soul
May live at peace. He shall conceal it
Whiles you are willing it shall come to note,
What time we will our celebration keep   30
According to my birth. What do you say?
    Sebastian. I'll follow this good man and go with
        you
And having sworn truth, ever will be true.
    Olivia. Then lead the way, good father; and heavens
        so shine
That they may fairly note this act of mine.   35
                                        Exeunt.

                            Finis, Actus quartus.

21 deceivable deceptive. 24 the chantry by the chapel near by N.
26 Plight me . . . your faith N. 27 jealous jealous. 29 Whiles
until. note notice. 30 What time at which time. 31 my birth my
station.

Act V

SCENE 1

Enter Clown and Fabian.

Fabian. Now as thou lov'st me, let me see his letter.

Clown. Good Master Fabian, grant me another request.

Fabian. Anything.

Clown. Do not desire to see this letter.   5

Fabian. This is to give a dog and in recompense desire my dog again.

Enter Duke, Viola, Curio, and Lords.

Duke. Belong you to the Lady Olivia, friends?

Clown. Ay, sir, we are some of her trappings.   9

Duke. I know thee well. How doest thou, my good fellow?

Clown. Truly, sir, the better for my foes and the worse for my friends.

Duke. Just the contrary: the better for thy friends.

Clown. No, sir, the worse.   15

Duke. How can that be?

Clown. Marry, sir, they praise me and make an ass of me; now my foes tell me plainly I am an ass. So that by my foes, sir, I profit in the knowledge of

6 **This is to give a dog** N. 9 **trappings** train, attendants. 10 **doest** N.

myself, and by my friends I am abused. So that conclusions to be as kisses, if your four negatives make your two affirmatives, why then, the worse for my friends and the better for my foes.

Duke. Why, this is excellent. 24

Clown. By my troth, sir, no; though it please you to be one of my friends.

Duke. Thou shalt not be the worse for me. There's gold.

Clown. But that it would be double dealing, sir, I would you could make it another. 30

Duke. O, you give me ill counsel.

Clown. Put your grace in your pocket, sir, for this once, and let your flesh and blood obey it.

Duke. Well, I will be so much a sinner to be a double dealer. There's another. 35

Clown. *Primo, secundo, tertio* is a good play, and the old saying is 'The third pays for all.' The triplex, sir, is a good tripping measure; or the bells of St. Bennet, sir, may put you in mind, one, two, three. 39

Duke. You can fool no more money out of me at this throw. If you will let your lady know I am here to speak with her, and bring her along with you, it may awake my bounty further. 48

Clown. Marry, sir, lullaby to your bounty till I come agen. I go, sir; but I would not have you to think that my desire of having is the sin of covetous-

---

20 **abused** 'deceived' and 'wronged.' 20–3 **So that conclusions . . . for my foes** N. 29 **But that** but for the fact that. **double dealing** both 'double giving' and 'deceit.' 32 **grace** both 'Duke' and 'generosity.' 36 **Primo, secundo, tertio** N. 37 **'The third pays for all'** N. **triplex** triple time in music. 38–9 **St. Bennet** St. Benedict N. 41 **throw** throw of the dice.

ness. But as you say, sir, let your bounty take a
nap; I will awake it anon. *Exit.*

Enter Antonio and Officers.

Viola. Here comes the man, sir, that did rescue me.
Duke. That face of his I do remember well. 50
Yet when I saw it last, it was besmear'd
As black as Vulcan in the smoke of war.
A baubling vessel was he captain of,
For shallow draught and bulk unprizable,
With which such scathful grapple did he make 55
With the most noble bottom of our fleet
That very envy and the tongue of loss
Cried fame and honor on him. What's the matter?
1 Officer. Orsino, this is that Antonio 59
That took the Phoenix and her fraught from Candy;
And this is he that did the Tiger board
When your young nephew Titus lost his leg.
Here in the streets. desperate of shame and state,
In private brabble did we apprehend him. 64
Viola. He did me kindness, sir, drew on my side;
But in conclusion put strange speech upon me.
I know not what 'twas but distraction.
Duke. Notable pirate, thou salt-water thief,
What foolish boldness brought thee to their mercies
Whom thou in terms so bloody and so dear 70

52 **Vulcan** Roman god of fire and patron of metal workers. 53 **a
baubling vessel** a trifling vessel, an unimportant ship. 54 **unprizable** incapable of being valued, worthless. 55 **scathful** harmful.
56 **bottom** ship. 57 **very** even. **loss** those losing the battle. 60
fraught cargo. **Candy** 'Candia' and 'Crete.' 63 **desperate of shame
and state** reckless of shame and of his condition. 64 **brabble** brawl.
65 **drew** drew his sword. 66 **put strange speech upon me** spoke
to me strangely. 67 **distraction** madness. 68 **thief** 'robber,' a strong
word. 70 **dear** costly N.

Hast made thine enemies?
 Antonio.   Orsino, noble sir,
Be pleas'd that I shake off these names you give me.
Antony never yet was thief or pirate,
Though I confess, on base and ground enough,
Orsino's enemy. A witchcraft drew me hither. 75
That most ingrateful boy there by your side
From the rude sea's enrag'd and foamy mouth
Did I redeem. A wrack past hope he was.
His life I gave him and did thereto add
My love without retention or restraint, 80
All his in dedication. For his sake
Did I expose myself (pure for his love)
Into the danger of this adverse town;
Drew to defend him when he was beset;
Where being apprehended, his false cunning 85
(Not meaning to partake with me in danger)
Taught him to face me out of his acquaintance,
And grew a twenty years removed thing
While one would wink; denied me mine own purse,
Which I had recommended to his use 90
Not half an hour before.
 Viola.   How can this be?
 Duke. When came he to this town?
 Antonio. Today, my lord; and for three months before,
No intrim, not a minute's vacancy,
Both day and night did we keep company. 95

Enter Olivia and Attendants.

78 **wrack** wreck. 82 **pure** purely, only. 83 **adverse** hostile. 87 **to face me out of his acquaintance** shamelessly to pretend not to know me. 88–9 **And grew . . . would wink** N. 90 **had recommended** had given in charge, had urged. 93 **three months** N. 94 **intrim** interim.

Duke. Here comes the countess; now heaven walks
    on earth.
But for thee, fellow: fellow, thy words are madness.
Three months this youth hath tended upon me,
But more of that anon. Take him aside.

Olivia. What would my lord, but that he may **not**
    have,   100
Wherein Olivia may seem serviceable?
Cesario, you do not keep promise with me.

Viola. Madam.

Duke. Gracious Olivia.   104

Olivia. What do you say, Cesario? Good my lord.

Viola. My lord would speak; my duty hushes me.

Olivia. If it be ought to the old tune, my lord,
It is as fat and fulsome to mine ear
As howling after music.

Duke.   Still so cruel?

Olivia. Still so constant, lord.   110

Duke. What, to perverseness? You uncivil lady,
To whose ingrate and unauspicious altars
My soul the faithfull'st off'rings have breath'd out
That e'er devotion tender'd. What shall I do?

Olivia. Even what it please my lord, that shall be-
    come him.   115

Duke. Why should I not (had I the heart to do it),
Like to th' Egyptian thief at point of death,
Kill what I love? (A savage jealousy
That sometimes savors nobly.) But hear me this:
Since you to nonregardance cast my faith,   120

100 **but that he may not have** except what he may not have
(my love). 108 **fat** superabundant, unnecessary. **fulsome** offensive
to the taste. 112 **ingrate** ungrateful. **unauspicious** unpropitious.
113 **My soul . . . have breath'd** N. 115 **Even** monosyllabic. 117
th' Egyptian thief N. 120 **nonregardance** neglect, lack of regard.

And that I partly know the instrument
That screws me from my true place in your favor,
Live you the marble-breasted tyrant still.
But this your minion, whom I know you love,
And whom, by heaven I swear, I tender dearly, 125
Him will I tear out of that cruel eye
Where he sits crowned in his master's spite.
Come, boy, with me. My thoughts are ripe in mis-
    chief.
I'll sacrifice the lamb that I do love, 129
To spite a raven's heart within a dove. *[Going.]*

   Viola. And I most jocund, apt, and willingly,
To do you rest a thousand deaths would die.

                        [Following.]

   Olivia. Where goes Cesario?
   Viola.   After him I love
More than I love these eyes, more than my life,
More by all mores than ere I shall love wife. 135
If I do feign, you witnesses above
Punish my life for tainting of my love.

   Olivia. Ay me detested! How am I beguil'd!
   Viola. Who does beguile you? Who does do you
    wrong?
   Olivia. Hast thou forgot thyself? Is it so long? 140
Call forth the holy father.   *[Exit an Attendant.]*
   Duke.   *[To Viola.]* Come, away.
   Olivia. Whither, my lord? Cesario, husband, stay.
   Duke. Husband?
   Olivia.   Ay, husband. Can he that deny?
   Duke. Her husband, sirrah?

124 minion favorite. 125 tender hold. 127 in his master's spite
despite his master. 131 apt properly. 132 To do you rest to give
you peace. 135 mores customs. 137 for tainting for corrupting
(by feigning). 142 husband N. 144 sirrah 'sir'; the form is familiar
or contemptuous.

Viola.   No, my lord, not I.
  Olivia. Alas, it is the baseness of thy fear   145
That makes thee strangle thy propriety.
Fear not, Cesario; take thy fortunes up;
Be that thou know'st thou art, and then thou art
As great as that thou fear'st.

Enter Priest.

                              O welcome, father!
Father, I charge thee by thy reverence   150
Here to unfold—though lately we intended
To keep in darkness what occasion now
Reveals before 'tis ripe—what thou dost know
Hath newly pass'd between this youth and me.
  Priest. A contract of eternal bond of love,   155
Confirm'd by mutual joinder of your hands,
Attested by the holy close of lips,
Strength'ned by interchangement of your rings;
And all the ceremony of this compact
Seal'd in my function, by my testimony;   160
Since when, my watch hath told me, toward my grave
I have travel'd but two hours.
  Duke. O thou dissembling cub, what wilt thou be
When time hath sow'd a grizzle on thy case?
Or will not else thy craft so quickly grow   165
That thine own trip shall be thine overthrow?
Farewell, and take her; but direct thy feet
Where thou and I henceforth may never meet.
  Viola. My lord, I do protest.
  Olivia.   O, do not swear. 169

---

146 **thy propriety** thy identity. 149 **that thou fear'st** i.e. the Duke.
164 **a grizzle** gray hair. **case** sheath or skin, particularly of a fox.
166 **trip** trickery N.

Hold little faith, though thou hast too much fear.

Enter Sir Andrew.

Andrew. For the love of God, a surgeon. Send one
presently to Sir Toby. 172

Olivia. What's the matter?

Andrew. H'as broke my head across and has given
Sir Toby a bloody coxcomb too. For the love of God,
your help. I had rather than forty pound I were at
home. 177

Olivia. Who has done this, Sir Andrew?

Andrew. The Count's gentleman, one Cesario. We
took him for a coward, but he's the very divel incardinate. 181

Duke. My gentleman Cesario?

Andrew. Od's lifelings, here he is. You broke my
head for nothing, and that that I did, I was set on
to do't by Sir Toby. 185

Viola. Why do you speak to me? I never hurt you.
You drew your sword upon me without cause,
But I bespake you fair and hurt you not. 188

Enter [Sir] Toby and Clown.

Andrew. If a bloody coxcomb be a hurt, you have
hurt me. I think you set nothing by a bloody coxcomb. Here comes Sir Toby halting; you shall hear
more. But if he had not been in drink, he would have
tickl'd you othergates than he did. 193

Duke. How now, gentleman? How is't with you?

170 **Hold little faith** keep a little faith. 172 **presently** at once.
174 **H'as** he has. 175 **coxcomb** head. 180 **incardinate** possibly a
quibble on 'incarnate,' 'in the flesh,' and 'incardinate,' 'like a
cardinal' N. 183 **Od's lifelings** 'God's little lives'; a mild oath.
188 **bespake you fair** spoke to you politely. 191 **halting** limping.
193 **othergates** otherwise.

Toby. That's all one. Has hurt me, and there's th'
end on't. Sot, didst see Dick Surgeon, sot?   196

Clown. O, he's drunk, Sir Toby, an hour agone. His
eyes were set at eight i' th' morning.

Toby. Then he's a rogue and a passy measures
pavin. I hate a drunken rogue.   200

Olivia. Away with him! Who hath made this havoc
with them?

Andrew. I'll help you, Sir Toby, because we'll be
dress'd together.   204

Toby. Will you help an ass-head and a coxcomb
and a knave, a thin-fac'd knave, a gull?

Olivia. Get him to bed and let his hurt be look'd to.
          [*Exeunt Clown, Fabian, Sir Toby, and
                    Sir Andrew.*]

Enter Sebastian.

Sebastian. I am sorry, madam, I have hurt your
          kinsman ;
But had it been the brother of my blood,
I must have done no less with wit and safety.   210
You throw a strange regard upon me, and by that
I do perceive it hath offended you.
Pardon me, sweet one, even for the vows
We made each other but so late ago.

Duke. One face, one voice, one habit, and two per-
          sons,   215

195 **That's all one** it makes no difference. 196 **sot** 'fool'; possibly
'habitual drinker.' 197 **agone** ago. 198 **set** 'fixed' or 'gone down,'
i.e. 'closed.' 199–200 **passy measures pavin** an eight-bar double-
slow dance; F *panyn* N. 201 **havoc** N. 203–4 **be dress'd** have our
wounds dressed. 205 **a coxcomb** a simpleton. 206 **a gull** a dupe.
210 **with wit and safety** with intelligent regard for my safety.
211 **a strange regard** an estranged look. 215 **habit** dress.

A natural perspective, that is and is not.

Sebastian. Antonio, O my dear Antonio,
How have the hours rack'd and tortur'd me
Since I have lost thee!

Antonio. Sebastian are you?

Sebastian. Fear'st thou that, Antonio? 220

Antonio. How have you made division of yourself?
An apple cleft in two is not more twin
Than these two creatures. Which is Sebastian?

Olivia. Most wonderful. 224

Sebastian. Do I stand there? I never had a brother;
Nor can there be that deity in my nature
Of here and everywhere. I had a sister
Whom the blind waves and surges have devour'd.
Of charity, what kin are you to me? 229
What countryman? What name? What parentage?

Viola. Of Messaline; Sebastian was my father;
Such a Sebastian was my brother too.
So went he suited to his watery tomb.
If spirits can assume both form and suit,
You come to fright us.

Sebastian. A spirit I am indeed, 235
But am in that dimension grossly clad,
Which from the womb I did participate.
Were you a woman, as the rest goes even,
I should my tears let fall upon your cheek
And say, 'Thrice welcome, drowned Viola!' 240

Viola. My father had a mole upon his brow.

Sebastian. And so had mine.

216 **A natural perspective, that is and is not** N. 227 **Of here and
everywhere** of omnipresence. 229 **Of charity** in kindness. 233
suited dressed. 234 **suit** dress. 236 **dimension** form. **grossly ma-**
terially, in the flesh. 237 **participate** partake, inherit. 238 **as the
rest goes even** N.

Viola. And died that day when Viola from her birth
Had numb'red thirteen years.

Sebastian. O, that record is lively in my soul! 245
He finished indeed his mortal act
That day that made my sister thirteen years.

Viola. If nothing lets to make us happy both
But this my masculine usurp'd attire,
Do not embrace me till each circumstance 250
Of place, time, fortune do cohere and jump
That I am Viola; which to confirm,
I'll bring you to a captain in this town,
Where lie my maiden weeds; by whose gentle help
I was preserv'd to serve this noble Count. 255
All the occurrence of my fortune since
Hath been between this lady and this lord.

Sebastian. [*To Olivia.*] So comes it, lady, you have
                been mistook.
But nature to her bias drew in that.
You would have been contracted to a maid, 260
Nor are you therein, by my life, deceiv'd;
You are betroth'd both to a maid and man.

Duke. Be not amaz'd; right noble is his blood.
If this be so, as yet the glass seems true,
I shall have share in this most happy wrack. 265
[*To Viola.*] Boy, thou hast said to me a thousand
                times
Thou never should'st love woman like to me.

Viola. And all those sayings will I over swear
And all those swearings keep as true in soul

245 **record** memory (stressed — ´—). 248 **lets** hinders N. 251
jump agree completely. 254 **weeds** clothes. 259 **But nature to
her bias drew in that** N. 262 **a maid** i.e. a chaste man. 263
amaz'd dazed. 264 **the glass** the perspective glass of l. 216 above.
265 **wrack** wreck (the shipwreck). 268 **over swear** swear over
again.

As doth that orbed continent the fire 270
That severs day from night.
 Duke.   Give me thy hand
And let me see thee in thy woman's weeds.
 Viola. The captain that did bring me first on shore
Hath my maid's garments. He upon some action
Is now in durance at Malvolio's suit, 275
A gentleman and follower of my lady's.
 Olivia. He shall enlarge him. Fetch Malvolio hither.
And yet alas, now I remember me,
They say, poor gentleman, he's much distract.

   Enter Clown, with a letter, and Fabian.

A most extracting frenzy of mine own 280
From my remembrance clearly banish'd his.
How does he, sirrah?
 Clown. Truly, madam, he holds Belzebub at the
stave's end as well as a man in his case may do. Has
here writ a letter to you. I should have given't you
today morning. But as a madman's epistles are no
gospels, so it skills not much when they are deliver'd.
 Olivia. Open't and read it. 288
 Clown. Look then to be well edified, when the fool
delivers the madman. [*Reads.*] 'By the Lord, madam.'
 Olivia. How now, art thou mad? 291
 Clown. No, madam, I do but read madness. And

270 **orbed continent** N. 274 **some action** some legal charge. 275
in durance imprisoned. 277 **enlarge him** free him. 279 **distract**
distracted, insane. 280 **extracting** distracting. 281 **his** my remembrance of him (Malvolio). 282 **sirrah** 'sir,' used to an inferior.
283–4 **he holds Belzebub at the stave's end** he holds the devil
off N. 287 **it skills not much** it makes not much difference. 292
And if.

your ladyship will have it as it ought to be, you
must allow *vox*.

Olivia. Prethee read i' thy right wits.   295

Clown. So I do, madonna; but to read his right
wits is to read thus. Therefore, perpend, my princess, and give ear.

Olivia. [*To Fabian.*] Read it you, sirrah.   299

Fabian. (*Reads.*) 'By the Lord, madam, you wrong
me, and the world shall know it. Though you have
put me into darkness and given your drunken cousin
rule over me, yet have I the benefit of my senses as
well as your ladyship. I have your own letter that
induced me to the semblance I put on; with the which
I doubt not but to do myself much right, or you
much shame. Think of me as you please. I leave my
duty a little unthought of, and speak out of my
injury.   309

             'The Madly Us'd Malvolio.'

Olivia. Did he write this?

Clown. Ay, madam.

Duke. This savors not much of distraction.

Olivia. See him deliver'd, Fabian; bring him hither.
                          [*Exit Fabian.*]

My lord, so please you, these things further thought
on,   315
To think me as well a sister as a wife,
One day shall crown th' alliance on't, so please you,
Here at my house and at my proper cost.

Duke. Madam, I am most apt t'embrace your offer.

---

319 **apt** prone to, ready. 294 **vox** 'voice,' i.e. a loud voice or
the voice of a madman. 296 **madonna** my lady. 297 **perpend**
ponder, consider. 307–9 I leave . . . my injury N. 316 **a sister**
i.e. a sister-in-law. 318 **proper cost** own expense.

[To Viola.] Your master quits you; and for your
    service done him,   320
So much against the mettle of your sex,
So far beneath your soft and tender breeding,
And since you call'd me master for so long,
Here is my hand; you shall from this time be
Your master's mistress.
   Olivia.   A sister; you are she.   325

       Enter [Fabian with] Malvolio.

   Duke. Is this the madman?
   Olivia.   Ay, my lord, this same.
How now, Malvolio?
   Malvolio.   Madam, you have done me
    wrong,
Notorious wrong.
   Olivia.   Have I, Malvolio? No.
   Malvolio. Lady, you have. Pray you peruse that
    letter.
You must not now deny it is your hand.   330
Write from it if you can, in hand or phrase,
Or say 'tis not your seal, not your invention.
You can say none of this. Well, grant it then;
And tell me in the modesty of honor,   334
Why you have given me such clear lights of favor,
Bade me come smiling and cross-garter'd to you,
To put on yellow stockings and to frown
Upon Sir Toby and the lighter people;
And, acting this in an obedient hope,
Why have you suffer'd me to be imprison'd,   340

320 quits you releases you. 321 mettle quality of temperament.
331 from it differently from it. 334 in the modesty of honor with
regard for the propriety of (your) honor. 338 lighter lesser. 339
acting refers to Malvolio.

Kept in a dark house, visited by the priest,
And made the most notorious geck and gull
That e'er invention play'd on? Tell me why?

Olivia. Alas, Malvolio, this is not my writing,
Though I confess much like the character; 345
But out of question, 'tis Maria's hand.
And now I do bethink me, it was she
First told me thou wast mad; then cam'st in smiling,
And in such forms which here were presuppos'd
Upon thee in the letter. Prethee be content. 350
This practice hath most shrewdly pass'd upon thee;
But when we know the grounds and authors of it,
Thou shalt be both the plaintiff and the judge
Of thine own cause.

Fabian. Good madam, hear me speak,
And let no quarrel nor no brawl to come, 355
Taint the condition of this present hour,
Which I have wond'red at. In hope it shall not,
Most freely I confess myself and Toby
Set this device against Malvolio here,
Upon some stubborn and uncourteous parts 360
We had conceiv'd against him. Maria writ
The letter at Sir Toby's great importance,
In recompense whereof he hath married her.
How with a sportful malice it was follow'd
May rather pluck on laughter than revenge, 365
If that the injuries be justly weigh'd
That have on both sides pass'd.

342 geck fool, dupe. gull dupe. 349–50 presuppos'd **Upon thee**
put upon you beforehand. 351 shrewdly pass'd upon thee ma-
liciously been put upon you. 355 nor no 'nor,' an emphatic
negative. 360 Upon on account of. stubborn haughty. parts personal attributes, characteristics. 362 importance importunity.
364 it the plot. 365 pluck on draw on, urge on.

Olivia. Alas poor fool, how have they baffl'd thee!

Clown. Why, 'some are born great, some achieve greatness, and some have greatness thrown upon them.' I was one, sir, in this interlude, one Sir Topas, sir; but that's all one. 'By the Lord, fool, I am not mad.' But do you remember, 'Madam, why laugh you at such a barren rascal? And you smile not, he's gagg'd'? And thus the whirligig of time brings in his revenges. 376

Malvolio. I'll be reveng'd on the whole pack of you!
[*Exit.*]

Olivia. He hath been most notoriously abus'd.

Duke. Pursue him and entreat him to a peace.
He hath not told us of the captain yet. 380
When that is known and golden time convents,
A solemn combination shall be made
Of our dear souls. Meantime, sweet sister,
We will not part from hence. Cesario, come
(For so you shall be while you are a man); 385
But when in other habits you are seen,
Orsino's mistress and his fancy's queen.

Exeunt [all but the Clown].

Clown sings.

When that I was and a little tiny boy,
   With hey, ho, the wind and the rain,
A foolish thing was but a toy, 390
   For the rain it raineth every day.

368 **baffl'd thee** disgraced you publicly. 371 **interlude** an early form of dramatic comedy or entertainment. 374 **And** if. 375 **whirligig** circling course. 380 **the captain** Antonio, in jail. 381 **convents** comes together, suits. 386 **habits** clothing. 388–407 **When that I was . . . to please you every day** N. 388 **and a** ᵗhe *and* is superfluous N. **tiny** F *tine.*

But when I came to man's estate,
   With hey, ho, the wind and the rain,
'Gainst knaves and thieves men shut their gate,
   For the rain it raineth every day.   395

But when I came, alas, to wive,
   With hey, ho, the wind and the rain,
By swaggering could I never thrive,
   For the rain it raineth every day.

But when I came unto my beds,   400
   With hey, ho, the wind and the rain,
With tosspots still had drunken heads,
   For the rain it raineth every day.

A great while ago the world begun,
   With hey, ho, the wind and the rain: 405
But that's all one, our play is done,
   And we'll strive to please you every day.

[Exit.]

FINIS.

392–402 But when I came to man's estate . . . With tosspots still had drunken heads N. 393, 397, 401 With hey, ho, the wind and the rain F *with hey ho, etc.* 395, 399, 403 For the rain it raineth every day F *for the raine, etc.* 405 With hey, ho, the wind and the rain F *hey ho, etc.* 407 And we'll strive to please you every day N.

NOTES

[The Actors' . . . nearby]: A list of characters and the location of the scene do not appear in the First Folio. Rowe (1709) first gave the characters. Both the names *Orsino* and *Valentine* appear to have been suggested by a visit of Don Valentino Orsino, Duke of Bracciano, to the English Court in January 1600. Tradition and, less certainly, the text, make Sir Toby the uncle of Olivia. The name of Feste the clown is the contemporary form of *feast, celebration,* and is thus related to the title of the play.

Twelfth Night or What You Will The Folio spells the title 'twelfe,' the old form and pronunciation of the ordinal. Twelfth Night is the night of Epiphany, January 6, the twelfth day after Christmas. Traditionally commemorating the Magi and the manifestation of Christ to the Gentiles, the holiday marked the end of the Christmas festivities. The title may mean that the play was written for one particular Twelfth Night celebration, perhaps at court, or that the spirit of the play is consonant with the Christmas holidays. 'What You Will' simply enforces the air of lightness of 'Twelfth Night.'

Act I, Scene 1

1–3 If music . . . so die If music is the food for love, play on to excess so that love's appetite for music, having too much, may sicken and die. It is most improbable that the Duke is wishing that his love for Olivia may also die.

9–14 O spirit . . . in a minute O spirit of love, how alive and fresh you are in that, despite your power of receiving, you still devour things as does the sea. Nothing goes into love of whatever value and high esteem but that it falls into belittlement and low value at once. The central idea of the passage is the leveling power of love.

14 fancy In Shakespearean English the term has a number of meanings and is most commonly used in psychology and esthetics. The most probable meaning here is the imagination or the mind of the man in love.

108

18 the noblest His noblest *hart* (deer) and 'heart,' Olivia.

21 *hart* A second pun on *hart* and '*heart.*' The specific reference is to the story of Acteon who saw Diana bathing naked. As punishment, she transformed him into a hart and pursued him to his death with his own hounds. Shakespeare's most probable source is Ovid's *Metamorphoses*, Bk. 3, ll. 143–252 (Loeb ed.).

35 *golden shaft* Cupid had two arrows; one was of gold, had a sharp point, and kindled love; the other was of lead, had a blunt point, and brought dislike. See the *Metamorphoses*, Bk. 1, ll. 469–71 (Loeb ed.).

Act I, Scene 2

4 Elysium Viola picks a word that sounds like 'Illyria.'

15 Arion *Orion* of the Folio is either a phonetic spelling or a misreading of Shakespeare, the copyist, or the printer. The lines closely follow Ovid's account in the *Fasti*, 2, 113–16 (Loeb ed.). Arion, a bard on a voyage, jumped overboard to escape the sailors who would have murdered him for his money. A dolphin offered his back, and thereon the poet paid for his passage by playing on his lyre.

42 delivered Viola does not wish to be *delivered* or disclosed to the world; she is an unprotected woman in a strange country and she will remain in disguise until an opportune time for revealing her name and proper position in society.

61 to my wit The word has a large number of meanings in Shakespearean English. Here 'cleverness,' 'resourcefulness,' and 'intelligence' are the most probable synonyms

Act I, Scene 3

7 except before excepted The legalism, *exceptis excipiendis*, 'those things excepted which have been excepted,' was a phrase commonly employed in the writing of leases and allowed for conditions which had already been set up prior to the writing of the lease.

12 And Alternate form of 'an,' to mean 'if.' 'And' with this meaning is the standard spelling of the First Folio. 'An' is more common before 1600.

22 **ducat** The silver ducat of Italy was worth about 3s. 6d. in Shakespeare's time.

29 **almost natural** A natural is an idiot. Maria is punning on the word.

42 **parish top** Townships and parishes kept large tops which were made to spin by being whipped with eel skins. The origin of the practice may be in religious ritual; at any rate, there was communal top-spinning. See Alice B. Gomme's *The Traditional Games of England* (2 vols. 1894, 1898), 2, 301–3. Evidence does not support Steevens' statement that the purpose of the top was 'that the peasants might be kept warm by exercise, and out of mischief, while they could not work.' Nares' *Glossary* (ed. 1859) lists references but without confirmation of Steevens.

42 **wench** The use here is familiar, not derogatory.

42–3 **Castiliano vulgo** The exact meaning is unknown. Sir Toby wants Maria to be soberly polite to Sir Andrew. The Castilian people had a special reputation for politeness. Hanmer emended the phrase to *Castiliano volto*, which he glosses 'her most civil and worthy looks.'

49–55 **Accost . . . Accost** Sir Toby tells Sir Andrew to greet Maria; Sir Andrew does not know the meaning of *accost* and thinks it is Maria's name. Maria is a *chambermaid* (l. 51) only in the sense of 'lady-in-waiting' to Olivia.

70 **butt'ry bar** The buttery bar was the bar, usually in the cellar, where the butts or barrels of liquor were stored. The word is unrelated to 'butter.'

73 **It's dry, sir** Maria begins a series of puns with several meanings for *dry*, namely, 'witty,' 'in need of a drink,' and 'impotent' or 'old.' A moist hand was believed to be a sign of youth and of liberality in money and love. Sir Andrew misses the point, but Maria continues the pun with 'at my fingers' ends' and 'I am barren.'

85–6 **great . . . wit** The Englishman's diet was traditionally heavy and the quantity of beef in it was supposed to make him dull-witted.

93 **bear-baiting** An amusement in which a bear was tied or chained to a stake and unmuzzled dogs were set on it. The sport

was extremely popular among all classes and was commonly carried on in the theaters.

98–9 curl by nature Sir Toby is punning on 'art' as opposed to 'nature' and probably on 'tongs' (curling tongs) and 'tongues' in l. 97.

121 back-trick Minor verbal quibbles of an obscene sort probably occur in *caper*, *mutton*, and *back-trick*.

125 Mistress Mall's picture Attempts to identify Mall as Maria or as Mall Cutpurse, the criminal Mary Frith, born probably about 1584, are not convincing.

128 sink-a-pace The obvious pun on the word depends on 'make water.'

133 dam'd color'd There is no satisfactory explanation of the phrase. Rowe's emendation, *flame-color'd*, is commonly accepted. There is the possibility that *dam'd* may mean 'dark' or 'black.'

133 sit The two verbs 'sit' and 'set' were confused in Shakespearean as in modern English. 'Sit' is from Old English *sittan;* 'set' is from Old English *settan.*

136 Taurus The twelve signs of the Zodiac, named after astral constellations and related to time, were supposed to govern various parts of the human body. By consulting an astrological almanac the physician might determine the proper treatment for disease in a particular part of the body at a particular time of the year. The bull Taurus, according to some authorities, governed sides and heart; according to others, neck and throat. But Sir Toby's speech should not be taken seriously.

Act I, Scene 4

16 doors The plural is perhaps derived from the doors, commonly divided, of the Elizabethan house.

35 thy constellation According to astrological theory the character of a person was determined at the moment of his birth by the 'constellation' or arrangement of stars at that time.

41–2 woo . . . woo . . . would The quibble depends on the fact that 'would' was sometimes pronounced like 'wooed' in Modern English.

Act I, Scene 5

6 to fear no colors Maria's interpretation of the proverbial phrase suggests that *no colors* may have meant originally 'no flags,' and thus came from army usage. The clown is punning on 'collar,' the hangman's rope.

14–15 Well, God . . . talents May God let those who are intelligent use their intelligence, and may fools (both professional fools and foolish people) use their abilities. *Talents* means 'native abilities' and, by a pun on 'talons,' 'claws' or 'guile.' In addition, if Feste is using the northern pronunciation of *fools*, there is a pun on 'fools' and 'fowls' to match 'talents' and 'talons.'

20 away There is the remote possibility of a quibble on 'a whey,' that is, 'a turning sour' from the *summer*.

27–8 If Sir Toby . . . Illyria If Sir Toby would stop drinking, you would make as clever a wife (for him) as any in Illyria.

47–50 Anything . . . virtue Anything that is cured (and patched) is but patched; virtue that sins is mixed with sin, and evil that reforms is mixed with good. That is, all men are a mixture of good and bad. The clown is parodying formal logic.

51–2 As there . . . flower Every man is married to luck; when his luck is bad, he is betrayed, he is a cuckold. And beauty (Olivia's beauty) is transitory. The clown is saying that all men and women must resign themselves to fate.

58 motley The clown's motley was of pieces of cloth of different colors, or of a cloth woven of threads of mixed colors.

91 zanies The understudies, imitators and butts of the professional fools. The term is also a synonym for 'clown' or 'fool.'

96 no slander in an allow'd fool A fool who is allowed or privileged to practice his foolery (part of which is to insult people) cannot be guilty of slander.

122 A plague Sir Toby traditionally belches before these words.

150–1 sheriff's post . . . supporter to a bench Carved and painted posts were put by the doors of town officials. *Supporter* is used in the sense of 'prop' or 'post.'

167 SD Enter Viola The First Folio reading of *Enter Violenta* is a possible reflection of Italian background for the narrative but more probably a misreading by the compositor of 'Vlola enter.'

173 if this be A typical example of the present subjunctive, now more restricted in use.

185 my profound heart My deeply penetrating lady. 'Heart' is a common form of address to a lady.

202–3 'Tis not that time . . . dialogue The moon has not now influenced me enough to make me a party to skipping over and confusing a conversation. The moon was believed to produce lunacy, or moon-madness. The common addition of *so* after *in* is unnecessary.

206 giant The traditional guard of the lady in medieval romances. The word is applied ironically to Maria who is small. Other references to her size are *Penthesilea* (II.3.183); *little villain* (II.5.14); and *youngest wren of mine* (III.2.66).

238 in grain The grain was red dyestuff consisting of the dried bodies of the insect *coccus cacti.*

248 item The term, adverbial in origin, meant 'also,' 'likewise'; it was used for introducing a new article, fact, or statement in a formal list.

292 thou art Olivia in her soliloquy shifts from the formal 'you' to the intimate 'thou' as she thinks of Cesario and her love for him.

302 County's Words ending in *t* tended to keep the old plural and possessive in *es.* This fact resulted in the back formation, 'county.'

310 Mine eye . . . mind My eye has taken too favorable an impression (of Cesario) for my intellect to approve.

Act II, Scene 1

1–2 Nor . . . not The double negative is an emphatic negative in Shakespearean English, as in Old English and in modern dialectal English.

3–5 My stars . . . distemper yours The arrangement of the stars at the moment of one's birth was thought to determine one's future destiny. During one's life an examination of those stars would tell whether the time was propitious. Thus Sebastian is saying: 'The astrological interpretation of my stars is bad; my bad fate might perhaps infect your fate.'

Act II, Scene 2

SD **Enter . . . at several doors** The scene is near Olivia's house. The stage direction means that Viola and Malvolio enter each by one of the different doors at the rear of the Shakespearean stage. The usual stage had two doors, right and left, with a third possible entrance through the curtain under the balcony at the center of the back or inner stage.

28 **Pregnant enemy** 'Pregnant' to mean 'strong' is common before and during Shakespeare's time. In ll. 29 and 30 there is the possible suggestion of Satan disguised as a serpent to seduce Eve.

31–2 **Alas . . . such we be** The First Folio is commonly emended as follows: 'Alas, our frailty is the cause, not we, For such as we are made of, such we be.' The alterations are attractive but unnecessary to a satisfactory meaning of the passage: 'Alas, O, frailty is the cause, not woman; on account of the way that we women are made, since we are of that sort.' The two final clauses are close to repetitious, and the repetition of *such* is a rhetorical trick which obscures the syntax.

Act II, Scene 3

2 **diluculo surgere** *Diluculo surgere saluberrimum est*, 'To get up at dawn is most healthful.' The maxim is from the Latin grammar of William Lily and John Colet, first printed in 1549. The book came to be known as the Eton Latin Grammar, and in its numerous editions and revisions has been a standard text for English schoolboys into the 20th century.

9–10 **Does not . . . elements** It was believed that life depended on the correct mixture of the four elements of the universe, air, fire, earth, and water. Note the plural subject and singular verb.

17 **the picture of We Three** A picture or signboard at an inn with the heads of two fools displayed, and the inscription: 'We three loggerheads be.' The onlooker is the third.

27–9 **I did impeticos thy gratillity . . . bottle-ale houses** The meaning is obscure. By *impeticos*, the Clown means 'put into the pocket of my long gown or petticoat.' Clowns frequently wore long coats. *Gratillity* is simply an improvised diminutive

114

for 'gratuity.' The following is a possible paraphrase of the passage: 'I did pocket your small gratuity, for Malvolio's nose can soon smell out money; my lady-love has elegant tastes, and the Myrmidons (where we drink) are no cheap drinking houses.' That is, the Clown is saying that he can use the money. *Whipstock* is 'whip handle.'

40 O mistress mine The Clown's song, either by Shakespeare or by an unknown author, was first printed in Thomas Morley's *Consort Lessons* (1599).

57 To hear . . . contagion If we can hear with our noses, the fool's voice and breath are pleasant to listen to but bad to smell.

59–60 draw three souls out of one weaver Weavers were famous for their singing and their love of song.

65–6 'Thou knave' The words of the catch are: 'Hold thy peace, thou knave; and I prithee hold thy peace.' H. H. Furness in *A New Variorum*, p. 118, gives the words and music. The earliest printing which he reports is in *Deuteromelia* (1609).

77 Catayan Chinese, a person from Cathay. They were believed to be dishonest and shiftless.

78 a Peg-a-Ramsey The reference appears to be to the coarse and immoral heroine of an old ballad 'Bonny Peggy Ramsey,' the words and music of which are reprinted in Thomas D'Urfey's *Wit and Mirth* (6 vols. 1719–20), *5*, 139. For a discussion of the music see William Chappell's *Old English Popular Music* (2 vols. 1893), *1*, 248. The ballad begins:

> Bonny Peggy Ramsey that any Man may se,
> And bonny was her Face, with a fair freckel'd Eye . . .

Sir Toby is thus saying ironically of Malvolio, who is about to enter, that he is handsome, coarse, and immoral.

78–9 'Three merry men be we' The words of the song perhaps appear in George Peele's *The Old Wives' Tale* (1595), Act II:

> Three merry men, and three merry men,
> And three merry men be we;
> I in the wood, and thou on the ground,
> And Jack sleeps in the tree.

Furness in *A New Variorum*, p. 120, prints words and music.

80–1 **'There dwelt a man'** 'The Constancy of Susanna' is a ballad on the story of Susanna and the Elders:

> There dwelt a man in Babylon,
>   of reputation great by fame;
> He tooke to wife a faire woman,
>   Susanna she was call'd by name;
> A woman faire and vertuous:
>   Lady, lady,
> Why should wee not of her learne thus
>   to live godly?

It is reprinted in the *Roxburghe Ballads*, ed. W. Chappell (9 vols. 1871–99), *1*, 190–3.

87 **'O the twelfe day of December'** The phrase is probably from a lost ballad. It is unlikely that Sir Toby is misquoting either 'Musselburgh Field' (the suggestion of G. L. Kittredge) or 'The Twelve Days of Christmas' (the suggestion of I. B. Cauthen, Jr.) 'Musselburgh Field' begins: 'On the tenth day of December . . .'; it is reprinted in F. J. Child's *The English and Scottish Popular Ballads* (5 vols. 1882–94), *3*, 378–9. 'The Twelve Days of Christmas' begins: 'On the twelfth day of Christmas . . .'; it is reprinted in Cecil J. Sharp's and Charles L. Marson's *Folk Songs from Somerset* (5 vols. 1908–09), *2*, 52–5, 74–5.

105 **'Fairwell, dear heart'** From 'Corydon's Farewell to Phyllis,' a song in Robert Jones' *First Booke of Songes and Ayres* (1600), ed. E. H. Fellowes (1925), pp. 24–5. Sir Toby and the Clown sing snatches from the first two stanzas only:

> Farewell, dear love, since thou wilt needs be gon,
> Mine eyes do show my life is almost done.
> Nay, I will never die, so long as I can spy.
> There be many moe though that she do go.
> There be many moe, I fear not.
> Why, then, let her go, I care not!
>
> Farewell, farewell, since this I find is true,
> I will not spend more time in wooing you.
> But I will seeke elsewhere if I may find her there.

Shall I bid her go? What and if I do?
Shall I bid her go, and spare not?
O no, no, no, no, no, I dare not.

120 cakes and ale The traditional refreshment for holidays and saints' days.

121 St. Anne The mother of the Virgin Mary. The oath is colorless. Compare *The Taming of the Shrew*, I.1.243. Unconvincing efforts have been made to connect the Clown's use of the oath with St. Anne as the giver of 'wealth and living great' on the basis of an unidentified quotation in Robert Chambers' *Book of Days* (2 vols. 1863–64), *2*, 389.

121 ginger Used to spice ale, ginger was believed to reduce drunkenness. Ginger was also esteemed as an aphrodisiac.

123–4 rub your chain with crumbs As steward of the house, Malvolio wears a chain with keys. The chain survives on the wine steward in the modern restaurant. Toby tells Malvolio: 'Polish your chain with bread crumbs,' i.e. 'Get back into your proper place,' 'Mind your own business.'

130 as good a deed as to drink A traditional comparison.

144 a kind of Puritan Maria means that Malvolio is oversolemn and overpunctilious, two characteristics associated with the modern use of the word 'Puritan.' Sir Andrew misunderstands her and thinks that she has said that Malvolio is of the reforming or dissenting party in the Church, that is, that he is not a good Church of England man. Sir Toby then protests the harshness of Sir Andrew's judgment and Maria (ll. 152 ff.) explains that Malvolio is not a Puritan but simply a conceited fool. Malvolio has already (II.3.91–3) done something which no stage Puritan would have done: he has spoken slightingly of tinkers and coziers (cobblers), traditional mainstays of the dissenting sects. In point of fact, Malvolio does not conform to the type of the stage Puritan common in the drama of the period. Malvolio has the sobriety and the conceit of the stage Puritan, but in the further complexities of his character he goes as far beyond the stock figure as Falstaff goes beyond the *miles gloriosus*, the conventional braggart soldier of Roman comedy.

155 swarths A 'swarth' or 'swath' is the space covered by the sweep of the mower's scythe in cutting one side of a field.

180 let the fool make a third In the plot Fabian and not Feste makes the third. The change may be an oversight on Shakespeare's part, or an indication of revision.

Act II, Scene 4

34 worn Hanmer's emendation, *won*, is commonly accepted.

53 Fie, away Rowe's emendation, *Fly away*, is commonly accepted.

57–8 My part . . . share it My portion of death, no lover so true did share (with me).

70 pleasure will be paid The line is proverbial. See *The Oxford Dictionary of English Proverbs* (1948), p. 507.

73 the melancholy god Possibly Saturn, but more probably the Clown is only saying that the Duke enjoys his melancholy.

75–8 I would have . . . voyage of nothing I would have men of such fickleness make a voyage, that they might have business everywhere and intend to go everywhere; for that's what always brings back a good cargo of nothing. I.e. if you aim at everything, you achieve nothing.

89 I cannot The next line, 'Sooth, but you must [be so answer'd],' justifies the emendation.

94–5 woman's sides Can bide Note the omission of the relative, common in early Modern English.

99–100 No motion . . . and revolt No genuine movement of the liver, the seat of true love, but a mere physical sensation in the palate which is subject to excess, satiety, and disgust. The singular subject with a plural verb is not uncommon in Shakespearean English.

114–16 And with . . . smiling at grief Green and yellow are colors commonly associated with sadness and decay. The sense of the passage is that Viola's sister sat calmly, like a statue of Patience, and smiled in the midst of her grief. It is possible that the figure of Patience was suggested by Chaucer's *Parliament of Fowls*, ll. 242–3:

> Dame Pacience syttynge there I fond,
> With face pale, upon an hil of sond . . .

Both Viola's sister and Chaucer's Patience are pale and are

seated. In addition, Griselda of Chaucer's 'Clerk's Tale' is a monumental figure of patience in the face of suffering similar to that of Viola's sister.

118 Our shows . . . will Our display of love is more than our actual will to love.

Act II, Scene 5

2 a scruple Literally, one twenty-fourth of an ounce, apothecaries' weight.

3 let me . . . melancholy The sense of the passage hinges on a pun. 'Boil' and 'bile' were pronounced alike, and black bile produced melancholy. The point may be that poisoners were boiled to death, but that melancholy was a cold and not a hot humor.

7–9 You know . . . a bear-baiting here Malvolio's dislike of bear-baiting connects him with the satirical portrayals of Puritans. But the trait does not make him a dissenter; it only emphasizes his puritanical or 'precise' mien.

14–15 my metal of India The East Indies were the fabled source for gold in the period. The First Folio reads *Mettle*, a common variant of 'metal.' There is probably a pun on 'metal' and 'mettle.'

23 trout . . . tickling It was believed that trout could be caught by tickling them about the gills.

27 complexion The mixture of the four humors, blood, bile, black bile, and phlegm, in the body. The predominance of one humor produced a personality of that humor. Thus the Duke Orsino might be said to be melancholic because of a predominance of black bile.

35 Toby This line and Sir Toby's 'Peace, peace' (l. 39) are commonly assigned to Fabian.

40–1 The Lady of the Strachy Her identity is unknown, and no satisfactory emendation of *Strachy* has been suggested. The meaning of the passage is obvious: Malvolio has in mind some story of a lady of high position who married one of the servants. The following are the more important of the emendations which have been proposed: *Trachy* or Thrace (Warburton); *starchy* or linen (Stevens); *Tragedy* (Bulloch); *county* (Kinnear); *Malfi*, or the Duchess of Malfi (Dunlap and Luce). However, Charles J. Sisson has discovered evidence suggesting that the reference is satirical and to the King's Revels company, and that it was interpolated after 1616.

42 **Fie on him, Jezebel** 'Fie' is an exclamation of disgust. Sir Andrew says: 'Fie on Malvolio, who is a Jezebel.' Jezebel was the haughty wife of Ahab. See 1 Kings 16 and 19 and 2 Kings 9.

54 **a demure travel of regard** Here and elsewhere Malvolio's English is pedantically heavy.

61 **my— some rich jewel** The dash is a necessary addition to the unpunctuated phrase in the First Folio. Malvolio is about to say 'my chain.'

64–5 **with cars** The reference appears to be to a method of torture or execution in which the victim was bound to cars or carts which then went in opposite directions. Compare '. . . but a team of horse shall not pluck that from me,' in *Two Gentlemen of Verona*, III.1. 265, or the phrase, current to the present, 'Wild horses cannot get that out of me.'

84 **woodcock . . . gin** The woodcock was proverbially a stupid bird which walked easily into the gin or snare. *Gin* is a shortened form of 'engine.'

85–6 **the spirit . . . to him** May the spirit of whims suggest to him that he read it aloud. *Humors* here does not seem to have the usual medical meaning, nor does it mean 'wit' or 'merriment.'

88–9 **her very C's . . . P's** Malvolio happens to spell out two Elizabethan obscenities. There are no C's or P's in the address of the letter as he reads it.

93–4 **By your leave, wax** The letter would be folded upon itself and sealed, and would have no envelope. Malvolio apologetically asks the seal for permission to break it. The request is conventional.

94 **Lucrece** The beautiful and chaste wife of Tarquinius Collatinus was raped by Sextus, son of Tarquin, king of Rome. Lucrece told her father and her husband of what had happened and then committed suicide. The story is the subject of Shakespeare's poem, *The Rape of Lucrece* (1594).

102–3 **The numbers alter'd** *Numbers* may be a contraction of 'number is.'

105 brock The more common phrase is 'stinking brock.' There is also a tradition that the badger is conceited and noisy.

110 fustian Originally a coarse cloth made of cotton and flax.

115 And with . . . at it The falcon—here a *staniel* or inferior kind of hawk—*checks* when it leaves the pursuit of the game it has been sent after and follows other prey. Sir Toby is saying: 'How quickly the fool leaves the truth and goes off on a false trail.'

124–5 Sowter . . . fox The dog will bark on the trail, however, though the deception is as plain as the smell of a fox. 'Souter' or 'sowter' means 'maker or mender of shoes' and is used of any bungler, botcher, or ignorant workman. *Sowter* is here the name of the bungling dog.

129 faults Fabian is punning. He means not only 'breaks in the scent' but also that Malvolio is excellent at getting himself into *faults* or difficulties.

130–1 But then . . . probation But there is no consistency in what follows. It becomes strained under testing.

133 And O shall end And the trick will end with Malvolio's exclaiming 'O' in disgust. Obscure verbal quibbles of an indecent sort occur from l.131 through 136.

136 any eye behind you It is unlikely that there is here any reference, as some editors have supposed, to Chaucer's figure of Prudence with three eyes (*Troilus and Cressida*, bk. V, ll. 744–5):

> Prudence, allas, oon of thyne eyen thre
> Me lakked alwey, ere that I come here!

140–1 and yet . . . bow to me And yet, if I were to force the meaning of this 'M. O. A. I' a little, it would indicate me.

145 born . . . achieve The emendations make the passage consistent with III.4.43 and 45, and with V.1.369.

148–9 cast . . . fresh Cast off your humble manner as a snake casts off his old skin, and appear new.

151 tang . . . state Sound out with theories of statecraft. *Tang* also means 'to taste,' 'to smack.'

154 cross-garter'd The garters held up the stockings or attached the breeches to the stockings. Cross-gartering was an eccentric fashion in which the garters were crossed both above and below the knee.

158 alter services In addition to the 'services' of the steward, it may be that Maria has cleverly suggested the 'services' of the courtly lover to his lady.

159–61 Fortunate-Unhappy Compare 'Fortunatus Infelix,' a common posy or short motto used as an inscription for a ring, picture, poem, or emblem.

162 politic authors The *pollticke* of the Folio possibly indicates the pronunciation.

173 Jove The use of the word here and elsewhere suggests alterations in the text after 1606 and that, consequently, the text of the First Folio is later than 1606. A statute of 1606 forbade the profane use of God's name on the stage. The Clown Feste speaks of Jove in I.5.115 and III.1.46, but the reference is appropriate to his intelligence and character. Malvolio's use of *Jove* and its use in several other places in the play (II.5.179; III.4.79,87; and particularly IV.2.12) sound strange or unnatural. It is probable that the original text read *God*.

182 the Sophy The brothers Sir Robert and Sir Anthony Shirley had gone in 1599 on an expedition to Persia. Sir Anthony had left Persia after five months; Sir Robert had stayed. An account of the trip appeared in *Sir A. Shierlies Journey Overland to Venice* (1600). The 'pension of thousands to be paid from the Sophy' may refer to reports of fabulous wealth to be had from the shah.

189 Wilt . . . neck Sir Toby offers to submit utterly to Maria's wit in the fashion of victims of military conquest.

198 Like aqua-vite with a midwife There is no certain explanation of the phrase. Either midwives used distilled liquor to induce labor, or midwives by tradition drank excessively.

Act III, Scene 1

20 wanton There is the remote possibility of a quibble on 'want one,' i.e. 'want a name.'

21–2 since bonds disgrac'd them I.e. since a man's word is no longer as good as his bond, mankind has been disgraced or put to shame by the formal and necessary pledges (bonds) imposed by law.

41 I would Shakespearean English, like modern American English, is not strict in the use of 'would' and 'should.'

43 your wisdom An ironic variation on the conventional title of address, 'Your worship.'

53–4 Pandarus . . . Cressida . . . Troilus Troilus, a son of Priam, king of Troy, loved Cressida of Troy. Cressida's uncle, Pandarus, acted as a go-between and Cressida returned Troilus' love. In an exchange of prisoners between the Greeks and the Trojans, Cressida was sent to the Greek camp to join her father Calchas who had fled to the Greeks. In the Greek camp Diomede courted Cressida and supplanted Troilus in her affections. Troilus and Diomede fought inconclusively, and finally Troilus was killed in battle by Achilles. Shakespeare's *Troilus and Cressida* was produced about 1602; he was familiar with a number of versions of the story, most notably Chaucer's.

57 Cressida was a beggar Robert Henryson (d. 1506) continued the story of Cressida in *The Testament of Cressid*. Diomede deserted Cressida who became a harlot in the Greek camp. The gods afflicted her with leprosy and she had to beg by the roadside. The victorious Troilus rode by, but he did not recognize her. She learned who he was and, after having sent him a ring he had given her, died.

76 encounter Here and with *taste* (l. 80) Sir Toby is playing pedantically with his words.

85 gait The *gate* of the Folio suggests that a pun was possibly intended.

101–2 'Twas never . . . compliment The world has never been a happy one since the pretense of humility (with the word *servant*) came to be a convention of polite behavior. The phrase 'merry world' has the force of 'good old days.'

113 music from the spheres It was believed that the universe consisted of a series of spheres, one inside the other, and all centered on the earth. The spheres revolved, carrying within them the various heavenly bodies, and giving off a divine harmony inaudible to man.

119–20 To force . . . none of yours That I forced on you by a shameful trick a ring which you knew was not yours at all.

121–2 at the stake . . . unmuzzled thoughts The figure is another reference to the popular sport of bear-baiting. The verb 'to bait' means 'to cause to bite.'

123 The line is irregular: it consists of an alexandrine (twelve syllables of six iambics) with an extra unaccented syllable at the end. J. Dover Wilson in his edition (1930) rearranges the lines:

> To one of your receiving enough is shown,
> A cypress, not a bosom, hides my heart:
> So let me hear you speak.
> *Viola.*   I pity you.
> *Olivia.* That's a degree to love.
> *Viola.*   No, not a grise;
> For 'tis a vulgar proof,
> That very oft we pity enemies.

125 Hides . . . speak The first syllable is accented and is followed by four iambics, a total of nine syllables. This type of headless line is common in the earlier drama and there is no compelling reason for regularizing it by emending *Hides* to 'Hideth.'

129 'tis time to smile agen I.e. it is time for me to smile once more and to forget you, if you are my enemy or if you can only pity me.

132 the lion . . . the wolf The lion is the noble Duke Orsino; the wolf is the cruel Cesario.

137 due west. Then westward ho Olivia's implication in the phrase 'due west' is that she is dismissing Cesario forever from her favor; she sends Cesario toward the setting sun. Cesario (Viola) answers with a more cheerful phrase, 'Westward ho!' The Thames boatmen cried 'Westward ho!' and 'Eastward ho!' to prospective passengers to indicate the direction of the next trip on the river.

142-3 That you do think . . . the same of you Viola says that Olivia thinks she is in love with a man, and that she is not. Olivia, not understanding the statement, and thinking that Viola has meant either that Olivia is not really in love, or that she is mad, answers that she (Olivia) believes the same thing of Viola ('you do think you are not what you are'), that is, that Viola really does love Olivia, or that Viola is mad to reject Olivia's love.

156-9 Do not extort . . . better Do not extract by force your arguments from the fact that, because I woo you, you have no reason to accept. But rather make your logic firm with this reasonable proposition: love which is sought is good, but love which is given unsought is better.

Act III, Scene 2

2 venom Here and elsewhere Sir Toby plays with words by using them out of their ordinary context.

7 orchard From Old English *ortyeard*. The first element *ort-* is probably from the Latin [*h*]*ortus*, 'garden'; *-yeard* is the modern 'yard.'

8 see The Folio is commonly emended to *see thee*.

18 dormouse The dormouse was traditionally a sleepy animal.

24 double gilt The *double gilt* or gilding (a double dipping or plating of an object by a goldsmith) was the opportunity, doubly golden, to prove superiority both as a lover and as a fighter.

26–7 an icicle on a Dutchman's beard The phrase may be connected with the voyages, famous around 1600, of the Dutchman Barentz to the Arctic regions in 1596. An account by Gerritt de Veer had appeared in Amsterdam in 1598 and was entered in English in the Stationers' Register in 1598 (ed. E. Arber, *3*, 118): '. . . A true description of Three voyages by sea . . . and of the feirce Beares and other Sea monsters, and marveylous could, and howe in the last voyage, the shippe is besett in Iyce . . . by Jerrett De Veer . . .'

30 Brownist A member of the religious sect founded by Robert Browne (1550?–1633?). Browne opposed both the Episcopal and the Presbyterian forms of church government and advocated the Independent or Congregationalist form. He preached separation around 1578–80, but he later submitted to the Church of England and for forty years was a rector in Northamptonshire.

44 If thou thou'st him 'Thou' corresponded to the French *tu* and German *du*, proper for addressing children, close relatives, friends, and inferiors, but an insult when used with strangers.

47 the bed of Ware The great bed of Ware is a 16th-century carved oak bed, ten feet nine inches square. It was one of the sights of Shakespeare's time and is referred to in a number of contemporary plays. The bed is now in the Victoria and Albert Museum, London.

48 **gall** An excrescence produced on the oak by the action of insects. Oak galls were used in the manufacture of ink. The pun is on *gall* 'bitterness.'

49 **goose-pen** The implication is that Sir Andrew's style will be silly.

53 **dear manikin** In the phrase there is the suggestion of 'puppet' or artist's lay figure to be twisted and manipulated at will.

61 **blood in his liver** It was believed that the liver was the seat of courage; blood in the liver produced courage. Compare 'lily-livered,' meaning 'cowardly.'

66 **youngest wren of mine** Sir Toby means that Maria is young and small in stature; the wren is a particularly small bird. 'My youngest little bird' is an adequate rendering of the phrase. The common emendation of *mine* of the Folio to *nine* involves the explanation that wrens lay from nine to ten eggs and that the last of the brood is supposed to be the smallest.

67 **If you desire the spleen** The spleen was believed to be the source of, among other things, laughter.

69 **renegatho** The spelling possibly represents an attempt to produce in the pronunciation the Spanish voiced spirant *d*.

78–9 **new map . . . Indies** The *new map* of the East Indies and North America was done in 1600 by Edward Wright with the assistance of Richard Hakluyt, author of the various *Voyages*, and John Davis, navigator. It is described and reproduced in *Shakespeare's England* (Oxford Press ed., 2 vols. 1916), *1*, 173–4. The *lines* which Maria speaks of are those of Mercator's projection, a system new to English maps of the period.

Act III, Scene 3

15 **And thanks . . . turns** The short line is commonly emended for scansion. The compositor or the copyist may have dropped part of the speech.

39 **the Elephant** A. C. Southern in the *Times Literary Supplement*, June 12, 1953, has shown that in 1598 'there was an inn known as The Elephant on the Bankside' and that an inn with

that name probably was there at least until 1605. The common London inn sign, The Elephant and Castle, survives notably in the underground station south of Waterloo.

Act III, Scene 4

20 this cross-gartering Malvolio now has his garters crossed both above and below the knee.

22-3 'Please one and please all' The phrase is common. However, Malvolio may be quoting specifically from a ballad entered in the Stationers' Register in 1592 (ed. E. Arber, *2*, 602): '. . . the Crowe shee sittes upon the wall: please One and please all.' The ballad was signed 'R.T.,' possibly for Richard Tarlton, actor and clown. It is reprinted in *A Collection of Seventy-nine Black-letter Ballads*, ed. Joseph Lilly (1867), pp. 255–9. The first stanza follows:

> Please one and please all,
> Be they great be they small,
> Be they little be they lowe,
> So pypeth the Crowe,
>   sitting upon a wall:
>   please one and please all,
>   please one and please all.

29 Roman hand There were two styles of handwriting in use around 1600. The old secretary hand, almost illegible to modern readers, was common. The Italian style (*Roman hand*), fairly close to modern script, was being used increasingly and was particularly popular with women.

36-7 At your request . . . daws The speech is ironic. Malvolio says: 'Should I answer the request of my inferior, Maria? Of course. Nightingales answer the calls of jackdaws or crows.'

55 made Here and in the following lines there is possibly a verbal quibble on 'made' and 'maid,' (servant). In addition, *madness* (l. 59) may have been pronounced almost like 'maidness.'

59 midsummer madness It was believed that midsummer produced insanity. Compare 'dog-days.' June 23, Midsummer Eve, was a time of magic.

74 **tang with** The *langer* of the First Folio is not recorded as a verb in the NED; and *tang* is in the letter which Malvolio is quoting from II.5.151.

76–8 **And consequently . . . and so forth** Malvolio stops quoting from the letter and seemingly explores its implications as to his future conduct for winning Olivia. There is the slight possibility that the sentence is a later interpolation.

78 **lim'd** Birds were caught by spreading birdlime, a sticky substance, on twigs or on trees.

90 **drawn in little** It is unlikely that the figure has the force of 'portrayed in miniature.' Devils were notorious for their ability to contract into a small space. The phrase would thus mean 'contracted.'

90 **Legion** Mark 5:8–9: 'For he [Jesus] said unto him, Come out of the man, thou unclean spirit. And he asked him, What is thy name? And he answered, saying, My name is Legion: for we are many.'

93 **How is't with you, man?** Wright assigned the line to Sir Toby.

106 **bewitch'd** Possession by a witch's spell and possession by the devil are two different things; in popular usage the two are interchangeable. Maria combines the two.

107 **Carry . . . woman** 'Take his urine to the wise woman for diagnosis.' A 'wise woman' pretended to cure disease, bewitchment, and possession by devils. In addition, she usually told fortunes.

121 **cherry-pit** A child's game in which the players throw cherry stones into a small hole. Sir Toby means that it is below Malvolio's dignity to be intimate with Satan.

122 **collier** The devil is associated with coal because of his blackness and possibly because of the traditional flames of hell.

140–1 **in a dark room and bound** The standard treatment for insanity. Whipping was also believed to be beneficial. Insanity was commonly regarded as amusing.

158–9 **A good note . . . law** A clever remark (since *scurvy* is vague) which keeps you from being legally liable.

203 **cockatrices** Fabulous reptiles hatched by serpents from cocks' eggs. Both the breath and glance of a cockatrice were fatal.

214 Goes . . . griefs Note the disagreement of subject and verb in the inverted sentence.

242–3 with unhatch'd rapier . . . carpet consideration with an unhacked rapier and for affairs of peace rather than of war. That is, when Sir Andrew was dubbed a knight his sword had never been used in battle, and he got his honor perhaps through influence, favor, or service at court (*carpet consideration*) rather than for fighting. The term 'carpet knight' is common in this derogatory sense. *Unhatch'd* is 'unhacked,' 'undented.'

257–8 unless you undertake . . . answer him Unless you undertake a duel with me, which with as much safety you might undertake with him in answering his challenge.

283 firago The substitution of initial *f* for *v* indicates a hyper-correct pronunciation, particularly common among speakers of southern English, some of whom tended to use, incorrectly, initial *v* in place of *f*.

286 hits *Feet* is perhaps regarded collectively; but 16th- and 17th-century grammar is frequently loose.

289 Pox on't The curse is a common one and refers to the great pox, or syphilis, rather than to the smallpox.

295 Capilet Diminutive form of *caple* or *capul* and derived probably from Latin, *caballus*, 'horse.' The word is common to Middle English and Icelandic.

314 the duello A standard work on the subject was *Vincento Saviolo His Practice* (1595).

370 image *Image* here means 'ideal representation' or 'ideal appearance' to be worshiped within the friendship code of courtly love.

373 vild There is commonly an excrescent *d* in words ending in *l* and *n*. Compare French *son*, English 'sound'; or the sub-standard 'drownded.'

378 empty trunks, o'erflourish'd The sense of the passage is that the devil deceitfully 'overflourishes' or decorates the empty bodies to give them a beautiful appearance. It is unlikely that *trunks* refers to ornamented chests for clothing. *Trunks* as 'bodies' continues the figure of the mind and the body from the lines immediately preceding.

394 hare The hare was traditionally a cowardly animal.

Act IV, Scene 1

15 a cockney The term seems to come from Middle English *cocken-ey*, 'cock's egg,' or a small and malformed egg. The various attached meanings are 'milksop,' 'a townsman,' and 'a Londoner.'

23 after fourteen years' purchase A normal purchase price for land was the amount of rent which would be collected from it in twelve years. Thus, *fourteen years' purchase* would be a high price.

39 You are well flesh'd 'To flesh' is to give a taste of the game killed to a hawk or hound in order to incite it further to the chase.

59 started . . . heart 'To start' is the hunting term for forcing an animal to leave its lair.

Act IV, Scene 2

2 Topas The topaz stone was believed to cure insanity; Shakespeare may have had in mind Chaucer's comic knight of 'The Tale of Sir Thopas.'

15 King Gorboduc A legendary king of Britain, Gorboduc's story is told by Geoffrey of Monmouth. The king is a leading figure in an early blank-verse tragedy by Thomas Sackville and Thomas Norton, *Gorboduc, or Ferrex and Porrex* (1562). The 'niece of King Gorboduc' is an invention of the clown.

20 SD Malvolio within The stage direction indicates that Malvolio is either inside the inner stage, a small enclosed area at the center and rear of the Elizabethan stage, or at the wicket of one of the doors at either side of the inner stage. The latter is improbable since he is the focal point of the scene. In a court performance he would probably be in a small house or 'mansion' made of canvas on a frame and set out on the stage.

45 the Egyptians in their fog Exodus 10:22 'And Moses stretched forth his hand toward heaven; and there was a thick darkness in all the land of Egypt three days.'

51 Pythagoras The Greek philosopher of the 6th century B.C. was believed to have been the originator of the doctrine of the transmigration of souls. The doctrine was common knowledge, but Shakespeare might have had it from Ovid, specifically from the *Metamorphoses*.

73 this sport to the upshot The *upshot* is the final shot in a

130

match at archery. *To*, Rowe's emendation, was either dropped from the copy or merged with the preceding *t* of *sport*.

75 **Hey Robin** The song has been attributed doubtfully to Sir Thomas Wyatt. It is reprinted in Percy's *Reliques* (ed. 1847), *1*, 196–9. The song begins:

> A Robyn,
> Jolly Robyn,
> Tell me how thy leman [lady-love] doeth,
> And thou shalt knowe of myn.

> 'My Lady is unkynd, perde,'
> Alack! why is she so?
> 'She loveth an other better then me;
> And yet she will say no.'

89 **five wits** The *wits* or powers of the mind were numbered five, by analogy with the five senses, and were common wit, imagination, fantasy, estimation, and memory.

103 **God buy you** The modern 'goodbye' is from 'God be with you.' Some variants are the following: 'God bu'y you,' 'God buy ye,' 'God buy to ye,' and 'God bu'y.'

104 **Marry** It is unlikely that the exclamation retains any of its original meaning of 'the Virgin Mary,' even in its use here with *amen*.

123–5 **I am gone, sir . . . again** The lines are possibly a fragment from a lost song. E. W. Naylor in *Shakespeare and Music* (1896), p. 190, assigns music to them.

127–33 **Like to the old Vice . . . 'Pare thy nails, dad'** The Vice was the comic character in the morality plays and stood either for a particular vice or for sin in general. He would sometimes *sustain* the *need* of the hero by helping him in his contest with the devil. The Vice traditionally carried a *dagger of lath* with which he would offer to pare Satan's nails. Shakespeare's fools are in a number of respects the descendants of the Vice.

134 **Adieu, goodman divel** An insulting and even dangerous way to take leave of the devil, since *goodman* was the form of address for a person below the rank of gentleman.

Act IV, Scene 3

24 the chantry by A chantry is properly a chapel devoted to the celebration of masses for the dead and supported by an endowment for that purpose. The term is used here in the more general sense of 'small church.'

26 Plight me . . . your faith 'Pledge me full promise of your fidelity [in the betrothal ceremony at church].' The actual marriage ceremony was frequently preceded by a separate betrothal ceremony which was regarded very seriously both by the betrothed and by the church. The marriage ceremony of the Anglican Church consists of a betrothal followed by a marriage.

Act V, Scene 1

6 This is to give a dog The following entry, for March 26, 1603, is in John Manningham's Diary, ed. John Bruce (Camden Society, 1868), pp. 148–9: 'Mr. Francis Curle told me howe one Dr. Bullein, the Queenes kinsman, had a dog which he doted one, soe much that the Queene understanding of it requested he would graunt hir one desyre, and he should have what soever he would aske. Shee demaunded his dogge; he gave it, and "Nowe, Madame," quoth he, "you promised to give me my desyre." "I will," quothe she. "Then I pray you give me my dog againe." '

10 doest The form is correct, but unusual in the First Folio which generally prints *dost*.

20–3 So that conclusions . . . for my foes The best of many explications of the passage is by J. Dover Wilson and Hardin Craig. The mock logic hinges on the fact that a kiss is made of four lips which are *negatives*. The lips are joined by two mouths which are the *two affirmatives*. The clown says that if conclusions are like this, then the conclusion that he is not an ass has only half the value of the conclusion that he is one. In addition to the obvious juggling of the words *negatives* and *affirmatives* in the parody of logic, there is a play on *ass* in the sense of 'professional clown' and *ass* in the ordinary sense of 'fool.'

36 Primo, secundo, tertio The term appears to come either from a game of dice (see l. 41) or from an undefined child's game, the philosophers' table.

37 **The third pays for all** Proverbial. See *The Oxford Dictionary of English Proverbs* (1948), p. 651. The meaning is probably: 'The third time wins all.' Compare 'The third time never fails,' 'The third is a charm,' and 'The third time's lucky.'

38–9 **St. Bennet** Any church dedicated to St. Benedict (480–543). There was a St. Bennet Hithe, Paul's Wharf, near the Globe theater. The church was burned in the fire of London in 1666.

70 **dear** In Shakespearean English the word is frequently no more than an intensifying adjective with the meaning of 'extreme,' 'serious,' or 'grievous.'

88–9 **And grew . . . would wink** And became as strange as someone who had not seen me for twenty years in the time it would take one to wink.

93 **three months** The fact that this is impossible by any time scheme that can be devised for the play is unimportant.

113 **My soul . . . have breath'd** Irregular grammar is common in Shakespearean English when the object precedes the verb.

117 **th' Egyptian thief** In the story of 'Theagenes and Cariclia' from the *Ethiopica* of the Greek Heliodorus, possibly of the 3d century A.D. There was an English version by Thomas Underdowne, *An Æthiopian Historie*, published in 1569 (ed. C. Whibley, *The Tudor Translations*, 1895). Thyamis, an Egyptian robberchief in danger of capture, intends to kill his beautiful prisoner, Cariclia, with whom he is in love. In the darkness of the cave he slays another woman by mistake. 'And if the barbarous people be once in despaire of their owne safetie, they have a custome to kill all those by whome they set much, and whose companie they desire after death, or els would keepe them from the violence and wrong of their enemies.' (Whibley, p. 38.)

142 **husband** The word is used here and below in the sense that the betrothal ceremony in the chantry was the legal equivalent of marriage. There were two sorts of betrothal ceremonies, *sponsalia per verba de futuro*, and *sponsalia per verba de praesenti*. Under the betrothal de praesenti, the more binding of the two, the couple pledged themselves as man and wife from the moment of the betrothal—the agreement is of the present. That a betrothal de praesenti has taken place is indicated by the use of the word *husband*. The couple are husband and wife although

they will not actually be married in the church until the marriage ceremony takes place at a later date. Edward R. Hardy, Jr., has observed to the editor that the priest in his speech, ll. 155–60, seems to echo the proclamation of the marriage from the Book of Common Prayer with the phrases 'joinder of your hands' and 'interchangement of your rings.' Finally, Sebastian says *betroth'd* in l. 262; and Olivia in ll. 317–18 clearly speaks of the double marriage ceremony to be performed at her house in the future. For an account of the two kinds of betrothals and the canon law on each, see George E. Howard's *A History of Matrimonial Institutions* (3 vols. Chicago and London, 1904), *1*, 313–20, 337–63.

166 trip The sense is 'you will trip yourself up.' The term is perhaps from wrestling.

180 incardinate It seems unlikely that the word is a pointless verbal blunder from Sir Andrew. If there is a quibble on *incardinate*, 'to institute to a cardinalship' and 'devil incarnate,' the line is an example of the anti-Roman Catholic jest, common in the English drama of the period.

199–200 passy measures pavin The *panyn* of the Folio appears to be a misprint for *pavin*. The clown has just said that the surgeon is drunk and has been since 'eight i' th' morning.' Sir Toby's phrase 'a passy measures pavin' is a reference to dancing, perhaps suggested by the word *eight* from the clown. 'Passy measures' is Sir Toby's variant on 'passemeasure' from the Italian *passemezzo*, a slow dance. The tune consists of 'strains' which contain an even number of bars, most commonly eight. The same structure holds for the 'pavin' or, as it is more commonly spelled, 'pavan.' The pavan is a slow dance of Italian or Spanish origin. The name is perhaps from the Spanish *pavo*, 'peacock.' Thus, when the clown tells Sir Toby that the surgeon was drunk at 'eight i' th' morning,' Sir Toby answers: 'Then he's a rogue, and he's an eight-bar double-slow dance.' I.e. he's a laggard and should hurry up.

201 havoc Originally the signal to an army for the seizure of spoil and for pillage.

216 A natural perspective, that is and is not A *perspective* or 'prospective' was a glass made so as to produce an optical illusion or distortion from nature. By 'a natural perspective' the Duke means that here nature has produced the illusion and not art. The phrase 'that is and is not' means that although the two people are real, they are not really one and the same person as the various characters in the play have supposed.

238 as the rest goes even As the other facts (which you have just told me) make you my sister. Compare the phrase 'comes out even,' i.e. is consistent, logical, right.

248 lets 'Let,' 'to allow,' is from Old English *lætan*; 'let,' 'to hinder,' is from Old English *lettan*. The second survives in the phrase 'without let or hindrance.'

259 But nature to her bias drew in that But nature drew into natural course or line of inclination (*bias*), and corrected, that mistake which you made of falling in love with a woman. The figure, a common one in Shakespeare, is from bowling; the balls were loaded so that they rolled in a curved line or 'bias.'

270 orbed continent Probably 'the sun.' 'As the sun keeps the fire that severs day from night.' But 'orbed continent' may also mean the curved path or sphere which, under the Ptolomaic system, is the course of the sun around the earth, the center of the universe. The meaning would then be: 'As the sphere of the sun keeps in place the fire of the sun that severs day from night.'

283–4 he holds Belzebub at the stave's end Belzebub or Beelzebub is loosely a synonym for Satan. The figure is from the game of dueling with staves or heavy sticks.

307–9 I leave . . . my injury I leave my duty of respect to you somewhat out of mind and instead speak from the consciousness of my injury.

388–407 When that I was . . . To please you every day Critical opinion of the Clown's song has varied from Warburton's 'This wretched stuff . . .' to Knight's 'We hold this song to be the most philosophical Clown's song upon record . . . It is the history of a life . . .' For a survey of the pronouncements, see Furness, *A New Variorum*, pp. 313–14. No earlier version of the song is known.

388 and a Furness states that the redundant *and* is common in ballads; J. Dover Wilson, that it is an insertion by the playhouse musician; Kittredge, that *and* carried a note of music.

392–402 But when I came to man's estate . . . With tosspots

still had drunken heads It is impossible, as well as unnecessary, to extract precise meaning from these lines. However, it can be argued that the following is the general meaning. The second stanza, beginning 'But when I came to man's estate,' says that his foolishness, which was of no account while he was 'a little tiny boy,' caused men to shut their gates against him, because they shut their gates against fools and knaves. The third stanza, beginning 'But when I came, alas, to wive,' says that after he got married he did not prosper because he was still a swaggerer. The fourth stanza, beginning 'But when I came unto my beds,' might mean: 'When I went to bed, like other tosspots, I kept having drunken heads.' But this interpretation necessitates the insertion of 'I' before 'had drunken heads,' and a strain on the use of the plural 'heads.' It is necessary to accept the song for what is; like much popular poetry, it lacks precise meaning, but it is roughly intelligible and a perfectly appropriate ending for the comedy.

407 And we'll strive to please you every day A conventional promise from the acting company to the audience, which might consist largely of regular patrons.

APPENDIX A
Text and Date

The earliest text of *Twelfth Night*, that of the First Folio (1623), is excellent: the spelling and punctuation are generally clear, and the lines offer few difficulties of meaning. The compositor has several times encountered words or passages which he did not understand, such as *staniel* (II.5.115) and *pavin* (V.1.200), and he fails to realize that Malvolio is reading from a letter in II.5.143 ff. The text appears to have been set up from a particularly accurate and complete promptbook; this conclusion is supported by the survival of a number of careful instructions: 'Enter Viola and Malvolio at several doors' (II.2.1), and 'Malvolio within' (IV.2.20), both of which indicate the construction and employment of the stage on which the play would have been produced. In addition the scene divisions, entrances, and exits are unusually complete. The copy is in all ways among the best of Shakespeare's plays.

John Manningham from the Middle Temple recorded in his diary for February 2, 1602, a performance which he had seen:

> At our feast wee had a play called
> "Twelve Night, or What you Will," much
> like the Commedy of Errores, or Menechmi
> in Plautus, but most like and neere to
> that in Italian called *Inganni* . . .

Within the play itself, the evidence supports Manningham. The song 'O Mistress Mine' (II.3.40 ff.) was printed in 1599 in Morley's *Consort Lessons;* and 'Corydon's Farewell to Phyllis,' from which Sir Toby sings the first line (II.3.105), appeared in Jones' *First Booke of Songes* in 1600. Fabian's 'pension of thousands to be paid from the Sophy' (II.5.182) seems to be a reflection of rumors of the moment concerning the fabulous wealth of the shah of Persia; the stories had started with the published report of Sir Robert Shirley's trip to Persia in 1599. The 'icicle on a Dutchman's beard' (III.2.27) sounds like a reference to the

Arctic voyages of Barentz, an account of which was entered in the Stationers' Register in 1598. The 'new map with the augmentation of the Indies' (III.2.78) seems to have been Edward Wright's, done in 1600; Wright used the Mercator projection (Maria's *lines*), then new to England. Finally, Valentino Orsino, duke of Bracciano, visited the English court in January 1600; and the Lord Chamberlain's men (Shakespeare's company) performed before the court on January 6, or Twelfth Night. The presence of Orsino's name in the play suggests that the first performance may have been on Twelfth Night 1600.

However, it appears that the text underwent revisions of an undetermined extent in the years immediately after 1600. In 1606 a statute was passed against the profane use of God's name on the stage; and *Jove* occurs in a number of places where 'God' would be much more natural. Sir Toby's 'Jove bless thee, Master Parson' (IV.2.12) is extremely strained; indeed, it sounds as though the revisions were intended to make the rule on profanity ridiculous. And Malvolio's 'Jove, not I, is the doer of this' (III.4.87) is inappropriate to the steward's character. Again, there is an indication of revision when the Duke asks Cesario to sing (II.4.2) and is told that Feste the Jester is not there. The song was probably first assigned to Cesario and, in a later performance, to Feste; the revisions of the script did not include the elimination of the old speech in which the Duke asked Cesario to sing.

APPENDIX B

Sources

The romantic plot of *Twelfth Night*—the story of the Duke Orsino, Olivia, and Viola—is derived from a large number of sources; it is not possible to name a single direct ancestor. H. H. Furness' variorum edition (1901) and Morton Luce's *Rich's 'Apolonius and Silla'* (1912) contain the most complete accounts of the versions, dramatic and nondramatic, from which Shakespeare might have drawn.

Shakespeare's immediate source for the narrative is unknown, not through lack of an earlier telling but because of the multiplicity of versions, a number of which seem to have furnished him with various details, ranging from bits of narrative to names of characters and, possibly, verbal elements for his lines. The mention, quoted above, in Manningham's diary of 'that in Italian called *Inganni*' is extremely ambiguous: he may have been referring to a single play which he mistakenly regarded as the immediate source of *Twelfth Night;* he may have been referring to a group of plays loosely known as the *Inganni;* or he may simply have been referring to the common dramatic theme of the *inganni*, that is, 'deceits' or 'tricks.' Finally, it is possible that he confused the word *inganni* with *ingannati*, 'deceived,' 'tricked.' There are three Italian plays with the name *Gl' Inganni:* the authors and the dates of printing are Nicolo Secchi, 1562; Curzio Gonzaga, 1592; and Domico Cornaccini, 1604. All three have plots which resemble the central plot of *Twelfth Night*, but it is unlikely that they are Shakespeare's sources. It might be noted that Gonzaga's play does have the name Cesare for the lady in disguise. The date of printing of the Carnaccini would perhaps have made it too late.

The probability is much greater that Shakespeare got elements for his story of the Duke Orsino in love with the Countess Olivia, and Viola, the disguised page in love with, and in the service of, the Duke, from the anonymous play, *Gl' Ingannati*. The title is sufficiently close to Manningham's *Inganni*. *Gl' Ingannati* was first acted in 1531 and was published six years later as part of the volume *Il Sacrificio,* a collection of assorted works dedicated to faithless mistresses and written by members of a Sienese literary coterie, the *Intronati.* One of the deserted lovers is mentioned by name, Agnol Malevoli, which might have suggested either Malvolio or Aguecheek. The action of *Gl' Ingannati* includes a brother and sister who look alike, and a trick of disguise by means of which the sister remains unknown near the man she loves. The ending is comic, with the proper transfer of affections and the solving of the mystery of the brother and sister. Among the characters there are a pretentious pedant, a dupe, and a nurse, possibly suggestions for Malvolio, Sir Andrew, and Maria. The lady in disguise takes the name of Fabio, certainly close to Shakespeare's Fabian, and in the prologue there is a mention of 'la notte di Beffana' or Twelfth Night. In short, the resemblances between the two plays are too numerous to allow the dismissal of *Gl' Ingannati* as a remote antecedent of *Twelfth Night.*

However, the connection between the two is not compelling simply because there existed in Italian, French, and English a number of versions of the same story; and Shakespeare is known to have been familiar with other writings of the authors of several of the versions. He had read, for example, the prose stories of Geraldo Cinthio, and in his *Hecatommithi* (1565) there is a retelling of the plot of *Gl' Ingannati.* Cinthio begins his version with a shipwreck, an event added to the dramatic version, and Shakespeare takes over the shipwreck, probably not directly, in *Twelfth Night.* Story 36 of the second part of Matteo Bandello's *Novelle* (1554) is again the story of the lady in love who disguises herself as a man, and of her brother who looks like her. Bandello has changed the names, but the narrative remains that of *Gl' Ingannati.* In Bandello there may be some verbal anticipations of Shakespeare. For instance, 'L'amoroso verme voracement con grandissimo cordoglio rodeva il cuore' perhaps suggest Viola's 'But let concealment, like a worm i' the bud, Feed on her damask cheek' (II.4.112–13). However, verbal similarities prove little about Bandello as a source for Shakespeare, since he is known to have been familiar with a French translation of Bandello. In François de Belleforest's *Histoires Tragiques,* vol. *4* (1570), there is another version of Bandello's retelling of *Gl' Ingannati;* and in the same collection there are other narratives which Shakespeare used for his plots. Belleforest keeps the names of the characters from Bandello, but omits and adds details to point up his narrative.

A number of other rewritings of *Gl' Ingannati,* all less notable, survive. Shakespeare may have been acquainted with the French play by Charles Estienne, *Les Abusés* (1543); but it is more probable that Shakespeare saw or knew about the production of a Latin adaptation, *Lælia,* presented at Queens' College, Cambridge, about 1595. Two Spanish plays are similar to *Gl' Ingannati.* They are *Los Engañados* (1567) by Lope de Rueda and the anonymous and undated *La Española de Florencia.*

But the version of *Gl' Ingannati* most easily available to Shakespeare was an English retelling in a collection of prose narratives by Barnabie Riche, *Riche his Farewell to Militarie Profession* (1581). The story, the second in the volume, is titled 'The Historie of Apolonius and Silla.'

In Cyprus the young and noble Silla fell in love with the Duke Apolonius, a guest of her father. Apolonius did not return her love and went to his home, Constantinople. Silla determined to follow him; accompanied by her devoted servant Pedro, who passed as her brother, she boarded a ship. The voyage ended in a shipwreck; all were lost except Silla, but she was thus freed from the unwelcome love-making of the captain. Silla saved her life by clinging to a chest which turned out to be filled with the captain's clothing and money. So she dressed herself as a man, called herself Silvio, the name of her brother with whom she was identical in appearance, and went unknown into the service of the Duke Apolonius in Constantinople. He sent her a number of times as messenger to the widow Julina with whom he was in love. Julina refused the attentions of the Duke, but fell in love with the young man Silvio and confessed her love to him. Meantime, the real Silvio, the brother of Silla in disguise, had arrived in Constantinople in search of his sister. Julina saw him, mistook him for the servant, and was betrothed to him; but he then left still in search of his sister. Julina presently found that she was to have a child by him.

When Apolonius learned that his servant Silvio had seduced Julina he threw Silvio in a dungeon. Later Apolonius attempted to compel Silvio to marry Julina; but Silvio revealed to Julina the disguise and her (Silla's) love for Apolonius. Having heard the story from Julina, Apolonius decided that he was really in love with Silla and they were married. The story of their love got to the brother Silvio, and he returned to Constantinople to see his sister. Apolonius took the real Silvio to Julina and they were married.

In Riche's version, a prose tale centered on narrative, there is very little characterization, and the events move with a looseness which would be impossible for the stage. Shakespeare has added details of character and a tighter plot to produce from the leisurely 'history' a dramatic unit of swiftness and point. In essence, the narrative consists of two combined themes of deception. The first is the story of the siblings who look alike and who cause a series of ironic complications on the stage until the final scene in which they appear together and solve the mystery for the other characters in the play. (The audience is at no point mystified.) This device Latin comedy had taken from Greek, and Shakespeare had used it in *The Comedy of Errors*. The second device, the trick of the lady in disguise as a man and serving her beloved without his knowledge, Shakespeare had used in *Two Gentlemen of Verona*. Within the more complex pattern of the narrative of *Gl' Ingannati* (and Riche's retelling), the two themes of deception are combined; in addition, the beloved of the lady in disguise loves another woman and sends his page, really the lady who loves him, as a messenger to his lady. Thinking the page is a man, the woman falls in love with him. Finally, the complications are resolved and the page, revealed as a woman, wins the love of her master. Both the trick of disguise and the shift in sex were peculiarly plausible to the Shakespearean audience, accustomed to boy-actors in female roles.

No source is known for the comic subplot of Malvolio and his tormentors, Maria, Sir Toby, Sir Andrew, Feste, and Fabian. But the subplot has pleased audiences more than the main plot; and the play has been known commonly by the false title of *Malvolio*. The two plots are connected by more than mere events.

Both hinge upon the original theme of *Gl' Ingannati*, 'the deceived.' If the lover, the Duke Orsino, is deceived, so is the lover, Malvolio; and so are, in one way or another, most of the other characters of the play.

APPENDIX C

Reading List

HENRY B. CHARLTON, *Shakespearian Comedy*, London, 1938.

HARDIN CRAIG, *An Interpretation of Shakespeare*, New York, 1948.

JOHN W. DRAPER, *The Twelfth Night of Shakespeare's Audience*, Stanford, Calif., 1950.

H. H. FURNESS, ed., *Twelfe Night, A New Variorum*, Philadelphia, 1901.

LESLIE HOTSON, *The First Night of 'Twelfth Night'* (1954?).

GEORGE L. KITTREDGE, ed., *Twelfth Night*, Boston, 1941.

MORTON LUCE, ed., *Rich's 'Apolonius & Silla,' an Original of Shakespeare's 'Twelfth Night,'* London, 1912.

MORTON LUCE, ed., *Twelfth Night, The Arden Shakespeare*, London, 1918.

THOMAS M. PARROTT, *Shakespearean Comedy*, New York, 1949.

G. C. MOORE SMITH, ed., *Lælia*, Cambridge, England, 1910.

J. DOVER WILSON, ed., *Twelfth Night, The Cambridge Shakespeare*, Cambridge, England, 1930.